Cutting to the Chase

Tom Joyner

Joyner Management Group

First American Trade Paperback Edition

Published in the United States of America

ISBN 978-0-9660088-1-4

Acknowledgements

I want to thank my wife of 52 years, Anne, for her patience while I was spending hours on research for my commentaries, more hours on a book I'm writing on my time with Senator Jesse Helms, and finishing this book at the same time. I can multi-task well. There were times when she insisted that I find a place to stop and go on the porch to watch our birds at their feeder stations and I followed along, but, in no time, I was winging it back to my trusty computer. Anne is a Conservative and truly tolerant.

I also want to thank my administrative aide, Lynette, who has been with me for more than 30 years and who helped get this book organized. Her personal growth over the years has been astounding and shows what an average, ordinary American can accomplish. First, when it's a necessity to feed your children and then when the enjoyment of self-confidence kicks in.

And last, but not least, I want to thank Mark Grady for his invaluable help in editing and formatting this book. I've known Mark for many years and consider him a true friend.

Introduction

I began this book at the request of those who listen to my commentaries on radio, streaming worldwide on the Internet and the growing list of listeners who get my commentaries by email each week. It took me almost two years to complete and, unlike my previous books, I decided to ramble.

Nancy Pelosi attacked President Trump because he did not visit Middle Eastern countries last May in alphabetical order. Nancy enjoys the grape and periodically puts her foot in her mouth, shoe and all. There is an unproven rumor that she suffers from athlete's tongue.

I move from topic to topic with wild abandon. These topics are in no particular order, and certainly not by alphabet. I may add additional thoughts on a subject I've already written about as those thoughts come to me. That's what I mean when I say I decided to ramble.

I'm still an average, ordinary farm boy from rural Wilson County, North Carolina. I don't put on airs. I always remember where I came from and the joys and sorrows associated with where I am now. If you find a grammatical error or a misspelled word, you have my permission to overlook it. Actually, I hired an editor to spot errors and so if there are complaints I'll forward them.

The comments in this book are mine. I have no ghost writer to help me resurrect the *Dreams of my Father*, as Obama did, or as Hillary did when selling us an idea that it takes a village to raise a child. Perhaps that is true, but when the admonition comes from the village idiot it loses its luster.

Hard core liberals and career Democrats will set this book on fire by page 35. After all, a full book of truth would have been too much to ask them to read and by scanning 35 pages they show us how tolerant they really are. By that time, I will have cashed their check and the joke is on them! (LOL)

Chapter One

Just as this book was about to go to print, the entire nation was brought to a halt after a relatively small group of people decided to descend on Charlottesville, Virginia to protest the removal of any Confederate memorial statues.

When a lone-wolf white supremacist drove a car into a crowd of counter-protestors, killing one, the liberal media had all it needed to create the image they have touted for some time; that America is one big, evil racist nation run by evil white men out to destroy anyone of color.

This issue is so inflammatory I do not believe it will disappear into the bottom of the pile of our 24-hour news cycle. Because of that, and the fact it is an issue that really illustrates how Liberals want to divide the country, in order to gain power, I decided to delay the book a few days to comment on this important issue of race relations in America and how the left is manipulating us with a false narrative.

Let me start with this: God gave me a white skin. That was his choice, not mine. I am not now a racist...never have been one...and far from someone who could be accused of white privilege. my ancestor came to America as an indentured servant. I am not afraid to say that I detest the Ku Klux Klan, the Nazi movement and anyone who considers themselves superior to others due to skin color.

I was among the first broadcast owners to develop radio stations designed for black communities. In all of those stations, I insisted on top notch studios and equipment to change the stereotypes of urban based stations. I insisted that anyone working in these stations avoid racism and work as a family....and they did.

Raleigh has 97.5 FM because I built it. Fayetteville has Foxy 99 because I built it. And the Greenville-New Bern broadcast market has Kiss 102 because I built it. They were all programmed to serve those area's black communities.

Anyone trying to pin the term racist on me will fail. Having said that, enough is enough. It is time for all Americans of good will; whites, blacks, Latinos, Asians; as well as Liberals, Conservatives, Republicans and Democrats to stop living in a fantasy world and grasp what they are doing to our country. And make no mistake, these protests and counter protests are planned and deliberate.

In September 2017, I will have been granted 75 years of life in America. I've had a long, challenging, but rewarding life, and I have no fear of the future. But, like many of you, I have great fears about the world we are leaving for our children and grandchildren. Moreover, thanks to liberal progressive political correctness, I have great fears of the young people we are leaving in the world.

Decades ago communism told us that they would destroy us from within. They set out on that long road and we are only now beginning to see the results of their work coming true.

As John Zeigler said in 2015, "We have gone nuts as a culture."

Proof of that was seen last week in Charlottesville, Virginia when a white supremacy group had a permit to demonstrate. Regardless of how much we disagree with the Klan, Nazis, and those who feel superior to others because of the color of their skin, these people had a legal permit for their march.

Counter protestors had no demonstration permit and yet they showed up to confront those who had been legally permitted to march. The claims that they brought bats, clubs, and homemade flame throwers with them only to defend themselves rings hollow.

If they had stayed at home or quietly watched the white supremacists foolishly march, they would have needed no defense. The great majority of both the protestors and counter protestors were from out of state and had come to Virginia looking for and expecting to find trouble.

...en President Trump said that both
to bear blame, liberals and the fake
.. ....ia pretended that only one side was to
blame. When there is only one side there is no
need for violence. This isn't about whether or not
white nationalists, Klan members or Nazis
should be accepted; obviously they should not be;
but this is America and we can't go around
confronting, challenging and attacking people
simply because we find them reprehensible.

Within a day of the events in Charlottesville,
a Confederate statute was destroyed in Durham,
North Carolina by an unruly mob, filled with
hate. Officials did nothing to stop the destruction
of property that had stood there since 1924.

There are people in America who do not like
Dr. Martin Luther King, Jr. and who are
offended by the statues of him. I'm not one of
those people, but should they be free to destroy
the statues of Dr. King? If not, why not?

Are we to tear down the Washington
monument? Dynamite Mt. Rushmore? And what
about all those schools, streets and monuments
dedicated to the late Senator Robert Byrd of
West Virginia., who was once a recruiter for the
Ku Klux Klan. Since he was a Democrat no one
has suggested destroying all the things named in
honor of Sen. Byrd.

The people memorialized in the statues lived
in a different time; a time when slavery was
legal. It matters not that slavery is offensive in
this modern era. That was a different era.

Slavery flourished thousands of years before the United States came into existence and it was especially intense among African tribes and Arab Islamists. This was obviously long before there were Confederate soldiers. Should we go dig up the graves of the blacks who sold the slaves?

We do not endorse racism by pointing out that when two sides engage in violence, neither side gets a free pass. In Charlottesville, there were two sides that engaged in violence...not one. In Durham, there was only one side, leftists, and yet they engaged in violence in the destruction of a Confederate statue and exhibited hate by stomping and spitting on the statue.

Insanity and mob rule seem to reign supreme now, with only very limited opposition. If you speak up against mob rule you're labeled a racist and bigot. How else can you explain an obvious lie like "hands up, don't shoot" inflaming black communities, but spurred on by the fake news media. The bias liberal media deliberately broadcast false information spurring many to protest violently for weeks in a nation where the president and attorney general were both black men.

Our national conversation is now completely dictated by emotion and ignorance rather than reason and facts. This gives the rantings of the worst of our population far more power than they remotely deserve. I have never once seen the Confederate flag used as a symbol of blatant racism. Is it possible that some people use it that way? Of course, but if the standard of erasing something from an allegedly free society is a few nut jobs using it for purposes we don't like, then we are simply no longer free and nearly everything will eventually be banned. The revisionist history and arbitrary enforcement of the politically correct rules is truly staggering. The Confederacy was far more complex than just being about slavery, or even treason.

Chapter Two

The vast majority of American citizens who died fighting on the side of the Confederacy did not own slaves and they did not think of themselves as traitors to their country. When Confederate soldiers readied for the ill-fated Pickett's charge at Gettysburg, they shouted for Virginia, not for slavery. How could a Virginian, or any other man living in southern states be expected to fight against their home state? That was the dilemma that faced General Robert E. Lee.

Perhaps the most dramatic proof that we are seeing the Confederacy in any remotely fair context is this quote from a public debate during that era, from a man who would soon become president.

"I will say then that I am not, nor ever have been, in favor of bringing about, in any way the social and political equality of the black and white races; that I am not, nor ever have been, in favor of making voters or jurors of negroes, nor of qualifying them to hold office, nor to intermarry with white people. And I will say, in addition to this, that there is a physical difference between the white and black races which I believe will forever forbid the two races living together on terms of social and political equality. And, insomuch as they cannot so live, while they do remain together, there must be the position of superior and inferior, and I, as much as any other man, am in favor of having the superior position assigned to the white race."

That was Abraham Lincoln, who went on to eventually free the slaves. Since he made those statements, are we now to destroy the Lincoln Memorial in Washington?

Another aspect of this reaction, which is really scary, is how quickly and dramatically both Republican politicians and corporate entities completed caved on the issue. The fake news media distorts reality and makes something a cause which appears to portray one side as good and the other side as evil racists. Liberals immediately swarm in unison under the guise of morality. Prominent Conservatives, fearful of the false narrative of racism sticking to them and eager to show the media how they are not one of the them, do not even attempt to stand up for the truth.

Conservatives quickly give credibility to the media's fake story while also removing all political cover for any other Conservatives who might be inclined to fight for the principle of the matter. The fake news media then easily portrays any remaining resistance to their false narrative as coming from nuts and racists.

As far as the corporate angle, obviously businesses should have the right to sell whatever legal product they want. But, the immediate and nearly universal repudiation of Confederate materials which they have sold for many years without incident has been particularly disturbing.

This entire controversy exposes how strong a hold political correctness, the belief that only the side of an issue that the fake news media is on is acceptable, now has our culture in its grips and how corrosive it has been to our freedom of speech in this country. Soon, "y'all" will be the new "n" word.

Chapter Three

Anti-White Racism

Anti-white racism is a world-wide phenomenon. The adherents of multiculturalism have allowed, and even encouraged, racism and hatred against white people, as well as creating an atmosphere of double-standards against the interests of white people, often hinging upon the multiculturalist-created psychosis of the white guilt complex.

Anti-white racism is generally quite acceptable in the fake news media. David Horowitz has pointed out the imbalance of tolerance in attacks upon those who use what others claim is hate speech. Basically, for the left, hate speech is any speech that they do not agree with.

The fact is that it is not okay in America to hate blacks, but it is okay in our politically correct culture to hate white people. Entire academic departments and college curricula are based on this idea. All white people are the oppressors of minority communities and cultures. There is even an academic field of white studies to parallel black studies and women studies.

Whiteness-studies academics have their own magazine published out of Cambridge, Massachusetts, the site of Harvard and M.I.T. The area is one of the most liberal communities in America. The name of that magazine is *Race Traitor* and its motto proclaims "treason to whiteness is loyalty to humanity."

Under the influence of the left, our universities have become purveyors of racial poisons, but the rest of the country cannot notice this because the targets of the hatred, whites, are not politically-correct victims. The agenda of contemporary leftists are merely updated versions of the ideas and agendas of the Marxist left that once supported the communist empire.

The same radicals who launched the social and political eruptions of the 1960s have now become the politically-correct faculties of American universities. Their goal remains the destruction of America's national identity and, in particular, the moral, political and economic institutions that form its social foundation.

In the fake news media, anti-black "hate crimes" are widely reported and publicized, while anti-white "hate crimes" are largely ignored and swept under the rug. Anti-white lyrics in black music are also ignored.

A white professor at Harvard university, Noel Ignatiev, published an article in 2002 entitled *Abolish the White Race, By Any Means Necessary*.

In that article, he said, "The key to solving the social problems of our age is to abolish the white race. We intend to keep bashing the dead white males, and the live ones, and the females too, until the social construct known as the white race is destroyed...not deconstructed...but destroyed."

This was quite acceptable to Harvard University, as it was presented as an attack on the cultural idea of "whiteness." Of course, if anyone were to publish an article entitled *Abolish the Black Race*, American cities would be set afire, stores looted and innocent white people assaulted or killed. Liberals call that being tolerant.

Language was a prime factor in the murder of six-million Jews by the national socialists in Germany and sixty to eighty million class enemies by communists in Russia and China. Today, similar language is being used in America's college and universities to annihilate the history, culture, and self-esteem of white people.

While teaching whites to hate themselves, diversity educators are simultaneously teaching people of color to hate white people. They teach that the privilege of the white skin can only be remedied by legal privileges for blacks; thus, the necessity of racial quotas and affirmative action.

Diversity educators also deny that our culture is being balkanized. What is really happening they say is the evil, racist white culture is being stamped out, and whites are finding a ne. existence as allies of the oppressed. Being called a racist can ruin a career just like Communist blacklisting could destroy someone in the 50s.

It is extraordinary that white taxpayers and donors are pouring billions of dollars into these re-education camps dedicated to the destruction of white consciousness. Parents, donors and trustees need to find some courage before the Nazification of our universities is complete.

The statement that 2017 America is the white Supremacist nation is not only the reflection of a deranged hatred for whites, but an act of hostility towards black America, whose opportunities and rights in this country are greater than in any other country in the world, including every African nation and Caribbean country governed by blacks for hundreds and even thousands of years.

Chapter Four

Black Lives Matter vs. The Real Facts

Black Lives Matter is a driving force behind the white supremacist ravings and is a roving mob whose premise is the claim that a systematic war is being waged on black people. That claim is deployed to justify riots in the streets, the burning of cities and open attempts to kill police. Remember their chant? "What do we want? Dead cops. When do we want it? Now!"

According to the co-founder of the Black Lives Matter Seattle chapter, Marissa Johnson, the phrase "all lives matter" is a new racial slur. Johnson's racial lies are easily refuted by the facts. While there are a relative few white crackpots, just as there are black crackpots, white America does not hate black children, and blacks are not being gunned down in the streets by whites or rounded up like Jews in Nazi Germany to be forced into prison slavery.

According to a study conducted by the liberal *Washington Post*, police officers who are black, Hispanic and Asian, as well as white, killed 662 whites and Hispanics, and 258 blacks. The overwhelming majority of all those police-shooting victims were attacking the officer.

Overall, there were 6,095 black homicide deaths in 2014, the most recent year for which such data is available. That's compared to only 5,397 homicide deaths for whites and Hispanics who constitute 80% of the population. Thus, it is true that blacks are being gunned down in numbers far out of their proportion to their representation in the population. But the truth that Black Lives Matter racists want to obscure is that almost all of those black homicide victims were gunned down by black killers. It is not whites who are gunning down blacks in the streets, but other blacks.

Moreover, 90% of the homicide victims of black killers are black. In other words, the real oppressors of the black communities are the Black Lives Matter movement and its Democrat party sponsors who are enabling a criminal element in inner city communities to terrorize law abiding black citizens, while crippling the efforts of law enforcement to protect them.

While blacks are only 13% of the population, they commit 38% of violent crimes. In America, blacks and Hispanics combined commit more than 95% of the murders. The war on police is a war to deprive law-abiding black citizens of their only real protection, since Democrat gun control advocates have already removed from the black and white populations of Chicago, Baltimore, and other crime ridden cities, much of their right to bear arms to protect themselves. Police officers are killed by blacks at a rate two and a half times higher than the rate at which blacks are killed by the police.

In line with all of this are the constant attacks from liberal Democrats, Republicans, in name only (RINOs), and the fake news media. Remember that these virulent attacks against President Trump began even before he took office. Every promise that Trump made to the American people and has tried to carry out has been demonized by these devious people. The whole idea is to keep attacks constant, spread the lies again and again and hope that the American people will become confused and accept the lies as real.

Liberal commentator Noam Chomsky once wrote, "People with power understand exactly one thing: violence."

His alt-left supporters must have been paying attention. As a result, the liberal cold war against the right has escalated from demonization to intimidation, harassment and violence, with Trump administration officials, Trump himself, and conservative members of Congress as prime targets.

The left's insanity has gained momentum from incidents during the campaign and turned it into an avalanche of crazy less than seven months into President Donald Trump's first term. In that time, we have had three riots in Berkley, California, and inaugural riots so bad that 200 people were charged with felonies. So called Antifa attacks on Trump appearances are now common and conservative speakers like Ann Coulter have to cancel events out of fear of violence from the left.

The hate against Donald Trump is unprecedented in presidential history. One liberal Tennessee woman was so upset over fake media hype about the health care vote that she reportedly tried to run Republican Congressman David Kustoff off the road. Left wing web sites rationalized her attack and made excuses for her violent behavior.

This latest outrage cycle was as predictable as the seasons. Liberals have spent more than a year trying to make Trump look like a lunatic combination of Hitler, Stalin and Pol Pot. They, and the fake news media, have so incensed the left's supporters that now they too have lost their minds.

The left's dementia has gone from tasteless, foul lyrics in songs to fantasies about blowing up the White House; or shooting Trump. But that was relatively tame by comparison to where we are today. Democrat representative John Lewis used a commencement speech to urge Massachusetts College of Liberal Arts graduates to "get in the way...get in trouble." The far-left and profane shock monkey Keith Olbermann even urged foreign intelligence agencies to target Trump because somehow America has become victim of a coup.

When you tell readers and viewers often enough that Trump is another Hitler and he's pulled off a coup, you are encouraging the unhinged among us to violence. It's long past time for journalists to pretend once more that they are neutral and stop trying to boost careers and leftist causes by taking down the lawfully elected president of the United States.

Donald trump was right not to jump to conclusions about Charlottesville before he had all the facts. Obama was not that tolerant and rushed to false judgment on several occasions. Trump condemned the violence within 40 minutes, but did not condemn groups by name without the facts. He is also right to blame both sides for the violence. Without the confrontation of the leftists against a lawfully-parading group there would have been no violence. It's not a matter of who was most at fault, only that both sides instituted and conducted violence.

For his honesty, Trump has had to endure the wrath of the fake news media, the race baiters of the black community, and even a handful of Republicans who fear being called racists and display no backbone against the hate from the left.

To claim that anyone pointing out the guilt of both sides in Charlottesville is a racist displays ignorance. I detest David Duke and all of those who claim superiority over people based on skin color. I can't be plainer than that, but, like the President, I will not overlook the hate and intolerance stemming from the other side. Neither should you.

This issue has become such an important, polarizing topic in America, I felt it was extremely important to delve into it at the first of this book. It is important to me you have facts not being shared in the liberal, agenda-driven mainstream media.

Now, allow me to share how I originally wanted to begin this book, with my own history. I hope it reveals how my life, work and family led me to be concerned enough for our great country to speak out against the threats to the future for future generations.

Chapter Five

I've been privileged to live a long life....longer than I imagined as a young boy growing up in rural Wilson County, North Carolina. I was the first of six children. My Mother died in 1990 of cancer and my Father died five years later of heart disease. Mom was 66 and Dad was 73.

On September 29, 2017, I turn 75 years old. While my parents have been gone a long time, I miss them both terribly and am so glad that I either called or visited them at least once a week.

The three of us began life in a small, wood-framed rental house at 1310 Goldsboro Street in Wilson. We were joined by my brother, Grady, who became known to all of us as Buddy, on December 1, 1943. Next came my sister, Ann, and three brothers; William, Johnny and Billy. Ironically, my two youngest brothers were the first to pass away, Billy died as a passenger in an automobile accident and Johnny's life was claimed by heart disease. Grady passed away in his sleep at age 73.

There is a reason I'm sharing a bit of my life story. I hope it reveals why I feel compelled to now be producing radio commentaries on what concerns me about matters affecting our great country. In fact, as you will see, my early years give no hint that I would eventually forge a broadcasting career that would span more than more than half a century and place me in the North Carolina Broadcasting Hall of Fame.

To the contrary, those early years were mired in poverty, family drinking, fighting sprees and a feeling of inferiority. My parents, John and Eva, were good people at heart, but they were overwhelmed by raising six children and the financial difficulties that came with that enormous responsibility. That led them to excessive drinking and even physical confrontations. These were scary events to a child. This led to screams and chaos among my siblings. I was the oldest, so I felt it was my duty to calm their fears. This meant I grew up fast. I didn't have an option.

For as long as I can remember, my father's brother, William, lived with us. That meant my mother and father had a third party to join them in turning weekends into a disturbing combination of alcohol abuse and disagreements. Uncle William was an alcoholic who eventually died of cancer.

I'm very thankful my mother and father did not suffer the lifetime fate of William. Two years after I left home and became a member of the United States Navy, my parents found the Lord. They gave up alcohol and cigarettes, joined a local church and dedicated their lives to God.

As hard as it was to live through their weaker moments as I was growing up, I could not be more proud of my mother and father for the dedication it took to put aside the booze and cigarettes; not to mention the abuse of each other. I'd give anything to be able to sit and talk with them again. My professional and financial success in broadcasting, which exposed me to a world I had never known existed, meant we had little in common. However, we did have genuine love for each other as family and a firm belief in God. I'm sure that's why we never lacked for conversation the rest of their lives.

Chapter Six

My days at Elm City High School focused more on sports than any education I was getting. After graduating, it didn't take long to realize I was ill-prepared for a job with any kind of real future. Frustrated, I turned to Uncle Sam and volunteered to become a member of the United States Navy.

In October of 1960 I boarded a plane to travel across the country and be introduced to the Navy ways at boot camp in San Diego, California. Whatever education I missed at Elm City High was made up for quickly. It was a move that changed my life. The Navy was a multi-level education for me.

First, I grew up at a time when schools were segregated. Now, I was in boot camp where I was being trained alongside people of various colors and ethnicities. Two of my shipmates were Ronnie Cox of Ohio and Clifford Williams from South Chicago. They were black men I was serving side-by-side with. We became a tight unit of young men with a common purpose.

The Navy not only exposed me to an amazing collection of people from all kinds of backgrounds, it also exposed me to wonders of a big world. From that on-the-job education, I learned Americans have opportunities and freedoms unlike any other place on Earth.

My time in the Navy introduced me to the fact not all education comes in a textbook. I realized I was at a disadvantage and made a lifelong pledge to myself I would do whatever I could to become a self-educated man. I also decided to take advantage of the educational opportunities the Navy offered to those of us in service.

I could easily see there are lessons all around us to be learned. We just need to be open to the free education. Unfortunately, many people make the same mistakes over and over. They didn't learn any lesson from the mistake. All of my business life, I shared that fact by warning my employees of having one year's experience 20 times.

After boot camp, the Navy gave me a job as a journalist writing for the base newspaper in Beeville, Texas.. The training for the work and the on-the-job training were very valuable. I began to gain more confidence in myself. I liked what I was doing and thought I could very easily see myself as a career Navy man. One accident changed all of that.

Just like in high school, I played sports in the Navy. I was on the base's fast-pitch softball team and played basketball for a team of medics. During a basketball game, I was on a drive to the basket when I fell. It was a hard fall and I was rushed to the base infirmary.

After completing some X-rays, it was decided I should be given a medical discharge. So much for a navy career. I had made many good friends on base and I was very sad at the prospect of leaving. I stayed two extra days just to visit with friends before having to say goodbye. As I left the base to begin the trip home to North Carolina, I had an eerie feeling knowing I had been a part of the base, had come and gone as I pleased, and that now I was an outsider.

I decided to save what little money they gave me at discharge and thumb my way back home. It was a long, slow trip from Texas back to North Carolina.

Chapter Seven

During the long journey home, a question was constantly on my mind. Now what?

I had maintained my commitment to continue my education, but I had no demonstrable job skills beyond my journalism training from the Navy. I quickly discovered there were no job offerings at local newspapers, so I found work on an assembly line. I used my off time to keep looking for a newspaper job. Finally, I landed a position at the *Evening Telegram* in Rocky Mount, N.C., with the less than robust salary of $70.00 a week.

Life in the civilian newspaper world was sure different than working at the base newspaper in Texas. I didn't get the same satisfaction, so I began to keep my eye open for any opportunities in a different vocation.

A girl I was dating at the time had a brother who worked as a disc jockey at a Virginia radio station. He gave me some advice. He said to get an FCC First Class Radiotelephone License.

The FCC first class ticket was what required to be an engineer at a radio station. During those days the FCC required every radio station to have an engineer on staff. It was quite a financial strain on small-market stations, but it was definitely a way to get into the business for someone who took the time to pass the rigorous test and get the license. Schools had sprung up around the country to teach a course on passing the exam. The courses usually consisted of six weeks of mainly memorization exercises and they cost about $600. I was living paycheck to paycheck with my small salary at the newspaper, so trying to raise money for the course was going to be a challenge.

I went about selling anything I owned that was not tied down. My ragged, old used car sold for a hundred bucks and I sold some other personal items and netted another hundred. I also was fortunate to learn the N.C. Vocational Rehabilitation office had granted me the $600 tuition to take the course after seeing my medical history that led to my discharge from the Navy.

Still needing a little more survival money to stay in Atlanta for six weeks, my girlfriend's father graciously co-signed a loan for $100 from his bank.

With everything taken care of, I was off to Atlanta and the Elkins Institute of Electronics. I was just young and naïve enough to have no fear as to what would happen if I failed the course or the test for the FCC license.

Chapter Eight

Thankfully, I didn't have to experience failure at Elkins Institute of Electronics. With a new FCC First Class Radiotelephone License in hand, I landed a job at a small-town radio station in Marion, Alabama. A man I had never met in my life had actually hired me over the phone.

Extra money was hard to come by in those days, so my parents borrowed $35.00 and loaned it to me for a bus ticket to a state I had never been to, to work for a man I had never met, doing a job I had never done. My job entailed a combo position. Not only would I be the official FCC-mandated engineer for the station, but I was also to be a disc jockey, the term used long before it evolved into "air personality."

When I stepped off the bus in Marion, I had a small cardboard suitcase with me and exactly $2.47 in my pocket.

Today, many young people could not conceive of making such a risky trip with little in their pocket. In those days, we knew when we had no choice. Plus, I had been raised with an attitude that failure was not an option.

I may not have realized it when I stepped off the bus in Marion, but I had discovered a field of work in which I would excel. I took every advantage I could to work with announcers I knew were better than me so that I could absorb their knowledge and techniques.

In those days being a radio DJ was a very nomadic lifestyle. You were always looking for a bigger station, better opportunity and a few more dollars a week. There were even jokes about DJs being U-Haul's best customers. I was no different.

After my first radio job in Marion, Alabama, I was off to work a series of jobs in North Carolina, Virginia, Kansas, Indiana, Colorado, Kentucky, South Carolina and Florida.

Eventually, I returned to North Carolina where I landed a job at a station in the small town of Benson. There, I had found not only a new job, but also met the lady that would become my wife, Anne Tart. We met on Thanksgiving of 1964.

I knew Anne was the one for me, so I proposed in December. I had a job waiting for me in California, but I turned it down to marry Anne. Our wedding day was April 25, 1965.

While I continued to take my career seriously, I applied the same dedication to my marriage. I wanted the best for Anne. We started our life together very modestly in a rented, single-wide mobile home just outside of Benson. It was still a paycheck to paycheck existence, but I took every opportunity I could to make extra money. I did remote broadcasts and voiceover work to supplement my regular salary. We both agreed we should go where opportunity took us, so, in true radio fashion, so, speaking of on the road again, we were in search of any better opportunities. We went to Kentucky, back to North Carolina, then to Florida and South Carolina. We again returned to North Carolina where I became the program director at WJNC in Jacksonville, N.C., the home of the Marine Corps Base Camp Lejeune.

By the time we arrived in Jacksonville, I began to realize being a disc jockey had a very limited future for a family man looking for success. With a few exceptions, you just don't see many 60-year-old DJs with financial independence.

For more than three years at WJNC, I worked hard and kept grueling hours. I signed on the station as the morning man at 5:00 a.m. and stayed on the air until 10:30. The last hour-and-a-half was a call-in show.

After my on-air shift ended, I handled the programming duties for both the AM and FM stations before hitting the streets as a commissioned salesperson.

In addition to my work at the station, I also landed work teaching a broadcasting course at Onslow Tech. On those nights, I didn't get to bed until 11:00 p.m. and had to get up at 3:45 a.m. to start all over again.

Believe it or not, that wasn't all I was doing. On weekends, I worked as a commissioned sales person for Columbia School of Broadcasting. They were well known in those days for correspondence courses for people wanting to get into the broadcasting business. I made enough from selling those courses to buy Anne and I our first home with a $13,500 down payment.

We settled into life in Jacksonville for the time we were there. In addition to working hard, I became active in the Jaycees and the Kiwanis Club. I learned how important it is to build a strong relationship in the community where you worked and lived.

During this time, a dream I had kept getting stronger. I wanted to own my own radio station. Thanks to two investors, that dream was about to come true.

Chapter Nine

The two investors who created the opportunity for me to own my own radio station put up the money for me to buy a station. If I met some specific sales goals, I would be awarded with one-third interest in the station.

After doing some research, I chose a station in DeLand, Florida, a town along Interstate 4 southwest of Daytona Beach and north of Orlando.

It wasn't an easy accomplishment, but in three years I had increased the station's advertising sales up to the point where we could sell the station and net a $300,000 profit.

While managing the DeLand station, a brutal lesson in life happened to me. It involved a young man I had originally hired during my first radio station management job in Kerrville, Texas. His name was Fred West and he had come into KERV radio seeking a weekend announcing job.

I have always been on the lookout for young people I could mentor and I believed Fred had talent to develop. He worked for me at the station before heading off to Texas A&M University.

After I arrived in DeLand, Fred contacted me and said he was not satisfied in college. He was wanting to work for me at the Florida station. I didn't want to be the man to discourage Fred from finishing school, so I consulted his mother before making a decision to give him a job.

Fred's mom said she trusted me and knew her son was not content in college. She said she had no problem with him coming to work for me in Florida. So, I hired Fred as the morning man at the station.

I imagine Fred and I caught quite a few glances when we stood beside each other. I am five-feet, six inches tall, while Fred stood six, nine and weighed 230 pounds. He was a gentle giant and my wife and daughter practically adopted him into the family. We all loved him.

Like me, Fred was ambitious. He was on the air from 6:00 a.m. until 10:00 a.m. and then would record commercials until about 2:00 in the afternoon. He could have left to go home at that point, but we never keep him out of the station. He loved the work and wanted to do anything to help. He was a quick learner and had a great deal of potential as a radio talent.

One morning, I was jarred out of my sleep by my phone ringing. I answered it and someone told me the station was off the air. It was 6:45 a.m. and Fred was one who was never late. I quickly got dressed and raced to the station to get it on the air. When I arrived, Fred was nowhere to be found. I called his apartment. No answer. I called another of the announcers and put him on the air. I decided I should go to Fred's apartment to make sure he was okay. I was not prepared for the series of events that followed.

I found the door to Fred's apartment ajar. I went inside and Fred was nowhere to be found. There was no sign of any disturbance. I went back to the station, wondering what was going on with a guy who was a dependable and likeable member of my staff.

Moments after I returned to the station I took a call. There was a male voice on the other end I did not recognize.

"Fred has been kidnapped. You'll be getting another call about the ransom."

The line went dead and I immediately called the Volusia County Sheriff's Department. They contacted the FBI. Law Enforcement officers quickly gathered at my office and we all awaited the call. It came quickly. I was told to put $10,000 into an unmarked bag and go to a phone booth located in at an area strip mall. When I got to that phone, I answered a call there and was told to proceed to yet another phone booth on the other side of town.

The FBI advised me to let them handle it from there. I feared for Fred's life and I insisted on taking the ransom money to the park myself.

When I arrived at the next phone, another call came in telling me to go into an area park and place the bag, with the money in it, above the towel rack in the park restroom. I pleaded with them to let me hear Fred's voice, but I was ignored. Instead, I was warned that I did not deliver the money, or if I insisted on speaking to Fred, he would be killed.

I did not know it at the time, but Fred was already dead.

As I had been told, I took the money to the park restroom and placed it above the towel rack. As I dropped the money off and was leaving the restroom, a man in a flowered-print shirt brushed past me and went inside.

An FBI agent had been crouched behind the front seat of my car the entire time. I returned to the car and told him about the man I saw entering the restroom. The agent directed me to drive to a spot where I could not be seen from the park restroom area. When I pulled up that location, the FBI agent left my car, instructing me to go back to the radio station and wait.

I later learned the FBI did apprehend the man in the restroom, but he ended up being just a stooge who had been paid to pick up the money. He didn't know the kidnapper, but gladly signed on to pick up the money so he could make a few bucks. He didn't know it was ransom money.

The FBI is very thorough. Everyone at the radio station was questioned, including me. They asked me if Fred had any enemies. I told them not that I knew of. When they went on to ask me about people who were in Fred's circle, I remembered a man named Perry Ables, who had befriended Fred and asked if he could stay in Fred's apartment while he looked for a place of his own.

With that information in hand, the FBI searched through Fred's phone records and discovered Ables had run up a large phone bill calling his relatives in Maryland. They found Ables living in an apartment of another unsuspecting acquaintance.

Ables eventually confessed to the kidnapping and shooting of Fred West. He told investigators that he knew how close I was to Fred and he was sure I would pay the ransom.

According to Ables, he asked Fred to drive him to a remote location where Fred's car became stuck. Ables then pulled a gun on Fred and told him his plans for the kidnapping and ransom. Ables said Fred lunged at him and the gun fired, striking Fred in the leg and severing an artery. The gentle giant still tried to run, but Ables shot him two more times, killing him. To this demented killer, Fred's life was only worth a $10,000 ransom.

I was devastated over what the law enforcement officers were telling me, but then I became almost sick when I heard the rest of the story. Perry Ables told them his original intent was to kidnap my daughter! He said when he realized my wife kept such close tabs on Lisa, he decided to go after Fred instead.

I testified at his trial and Perry Ables was sentenced to 25 years in a Florida prison. When he had a parole hearing, we contested along with Fred's sister. He served another three years before being set free. God only knows where this evil man is today and who might be in danger from him being free.

I've very rarely told this story about a sad and disturbing time in my life. In Fred's memory, I decided to share it in this book.

Chapter Ten

Despite the tragedy behind Fred's kidnapping and death, we were able to keep the station going and continue to grow. During this period of time, I learned a system of moving a station's transmitting tower to a location where it not only served its city of license, but also cover larger communities. That move alone would increase the value of the radio station, sometimes substantially.

Some of the stations I was involved in purchasing came with an FCC grant on hand to move the tower while other stations required my company to move the tower on our own, with FCC and FAA approval, of course.

When all was said and done, I ended up being involved in more of these stations, known in the industry as "move ins," than anyone else in broadcasting. Ultimately, I owned 57 radio stations in 13 states. They were around the country in North Carolina, New Mexico, Florida, Illinois, Virginia, Tennessee, Texas, Louisiana, West Virginia, Mississippi, South Carolina, Kentucky and Wisconsin.

All of these purchases and "move ins" were not a walk in the park. Every one of them came with the risk the FAA may turn down the tower move application. The sellers I bought some of the stations from knew there was the possibility the station could be moved and therefore wanted a price well beyond what the station was worth in its current location. It became a world of negotiation and risk when I made the purchase.

I knew I wanted financial security, but I also knew to reach that goal required not always working with a safety net and taking risks.

My approach to these risks was not taken with blinders on. I spent a lot of time researching and understanding the complex issues, costs and technical aspects of moving a station's tower and location. Understanding the details helped me make these station purchase decisions a bit more optimistically. Yet, the fear of miscalculation was always present.

Thankfully, my calculated risks paid off and my broadcasting company became more successful than I could have dreamed of. The success gave me the opportunity to find a nice home for Anne, especially since she had been with me through the days of starting out in a single-wide mobile home.

Anne and I bought a home in Naples, Florida in 1978 for $2.5 Million. That was a time when money was real. I don't mention the cost of the home to brag, but to make the point of WHAT hard work had brought us and how far we had come since I arrived in Alabama for my first radio job with $2.47 in my pocket. We had not only worked hard, but had eaten a lot of Spam and Hamburger Helper before the steak came along.

Not only had my business expanded since my humble beginnings in radio, but my family had, too. There was a daughter in the house.

Chapter Eleven

My success in radio ownership came with a commitment to be successful and that commitment was spurred on even more by an event twelve years before we bought the home in Naples. It was on December 8, 1966 that Anne and I welcomed Lisa Jane Joyner into the world in Danville, Virginia. It was certainly a happy day for me, but it also filled me with anxiety. I wanted to give my daughter a better childhood than I had experienced.

I foresaw the braces to come, a college education to pay for and material things I never had as a youngster. Having a daughter certainly pushed my dedication to make my business a success go up a notch.

Many parents who were raised in poor conditions and went on to achieve success tend to overcompensate in what we give to our children and grandchildren. In the process, we run the risk of making them complacent and expectant. We all felt we had no choice but to succeed in life. We had the drive and determination to make success possible. However, if we give our children and grandchildren everything, including what they would normally have to work for, it can take away the drive and determination to succeed that we had, or lessen it.

Despite my success and my desire to do all I can for my daughter, she became successful in her own right. Lisa graduated from Meredith College in Raleigh and married a young man from Doylestown, Pennsylvania who came south to attend N.C. State University and decided to stay.

Lisa and her husband have two daughters. Anna Marie, is an upcoming sophomore at her mom's alma mater, Meredith College, while Grace is an aspiring 9th grader. Both of our granddaughters have made us proud. Anna is on the Dean's List, speaks fluent French and is active in the Meredith College drama department. Grace is on her school's student council, runs track, is on the soccer and softball teams, all while working on the yearbook staff and maintaining straight As. We are definitely blessed.

I believe now that parents should do all they can to get their children through college or trade school. Once that is accomplished, especially if it can be done with no student loans to plague the graduate for years, the parents should not try to provide a cushion for life. That doesn't mean we love our children less, but that we realize they need to develop on their own, take responsibility and not depend on their parents. This should apply to our grandchildren, too.

We need to realize that when bad or hurt feelings develop later in their lives, the fault will be ours not the fault of our children or grandchildren if we have been the provider of everything for them. It is human nature to take the path of least resistance, which can lead to a lack of responsibility if we don't learn the lesson early in life.

In 1990, my mother developed cancer and we moved to Cary, North Carolina. We kept our home in Naples, Florida for more than ten years before selling it in order to settle near our daughter and her family in Cary.

Chapter Twelve

In April of 2017 Anne and I went to see a movie that had a profound impact on me, *The Case for Christ*. It's based on a true story of a man who was a committed atheist and wanted to prove the death and resurrection of Jesus was a myth. It was near Easter when we saw the movie and I was personally moved by a particular scene in the film.

The main character responded to his father with enormous anger. His father was old school and had been raised in a time when many men were taught not to express their emotions. The son thought his father never loved him or appreciated what he had accomplished.

After his father died suddenly, the son found a scrapbook his dad had kept with every article his son had written in the *Chicago Tribune*. It was only after his father died did he realize his father had loved him right until the end. The son was no doubt very regretful for the disdain he had shown his father.

This scene immediately brought back emotional memories of my own father, who had also grown up in a period where men did not show emotions. We all knew he loved us and sacrificed for us, but it wasn't until he lay dying in Wilson Memorial Hospital that he ever managed to say, "I love you, too, son." He uttered those words through ragged breaths. I had just said "I love you" to him. Then, it hit me. I, like my father, had never been able to say "I love you" to him, either.

At one point in my life, when I had reached a level of success in the broadcasting business, I mentioned to my mother that my father never seemed impressed or appreciated what I had accomplished. My mom told me my dad kept fading copies of newspaper articles about me in his billfold and bragged about his son to all he met.

I thank God I heard my mother tell me about my father's pride in me before he died. I didn't have the misfortune of having to learn the truth after he had gone, like the man *The Case for Christ* was based on.

In our youth, it's difficult to understand our parents or feel inspired to. We expect them to understand us instead. I vowed I would never hold back from telling my daughter and granddaughters how much I love them and how proud I am of their accomplishments. I've kept that vow, even during those times I felt unappreciated at home.

Chapter Thirteen

I entered the world of talk radio during a time when I can recall only one radio personality that was speaking out nationally. He was a firebrand names Joe Pyne and he originated his show from Chicago. I was at WJNC in Jacksonville, N.C., at the time and we carried his syndicated program.

He inspired and influenced me to the point of creating the very first talk show in the Jacksonville market. I called it "Ask Your Neighbor" and it aired from 9:00 to 10:00 a.m. on weekdays. The show became a local hit. There were so many sponsors wanting to advertise on the program that we expanded it, adding another half hour.

This happened in 1967, long before Rush Limbaugh or Sean Hannity came rolling into the radio scene. I've been engaged in talk radio, ever since I created "Ask Your Neighbor" 50 years ago.

Talk radio became popular in response to the domination of liberal network broadcast news and newspapers. Not all Americans are educated beyond mere intelligence, as liberals believe they are, but the rest have common sense and are well aware they were being subjected to bias news reporting. Newspapers run lengthy editorials on a subject and then limit the response of their readers to a few paragraphs. Thanks to talk radio, suddenly, the ordinary, average American could call into their favorite talk show and be given an equal opportunity to express their opinions.

The mainstream liberal media did not sit back and take this surge in talk radio sitting down. Their response was predictable. They attacked talk radio in general and personally attacked talk radio hosts. No lie was big enough for the elites to use against this new medium.

In 1994, I began a four-year stint as the afternoon talk show host on WPTF radio in Raleigh, North Carolina's capital city. WPTF was the state's second radio station and was a maximum power AM station, 50,000 watts. The station's reach was enormous and the station had a decade's old high reputation in the state. My show aired from 3:00 to 6:00 p.m. during what is known in the business as the important afternoon "drive time."

During my days doing the Tom Joyner Program on WPTF, my nemesis was the *News & Observer*, a newspaper owned by a liberal local family before being sold to the very liberal McClatchy chain of papers.

I have always found it interesting that talk radio has always used a delay system, of about eight to ten seconds, in order to prevent any profanity or false info from being actually aired. The host, or his producer, simply hits a "dump" button which brings the broadcast instantly back to real time, meaning the bad words or falsehoods are never heard on the radio.

In contrast, look how often newspapers, including the *News & Observer*, are having to print corrections for untrue statements or comments that have appeared in print. The editors and proofreaders have hours, not ten seconds, to catch an error, yet look at the number of falsehoods that get through.

During my show, I would review that day's newspaper before taking calls from listeners. I especially focused on their editorial page. The newspaper would respond with attacks on talk radio.

Today, the *News & Observer* remains a far-left-wing newspaper. There is a nasty cartoon in the paper almost daily about President Trump. Where were the nasty cartoons when Barack Obama was taking the country drastically to the left? Where were the nasty editorial cartoons when Hillary Clinton destroyed more than 30,000 e-mails after having been warned by Congress not to do so.

From radio stations in Texas, Florida, North Carolina, Virginia, Tennessee and Georgia, I have never taken my audience for granted. I love the give-and-take between us.

For more than fifty years I have spoken out for God and country. It has not always been easy, mainly due to the hypocrisy of liberals. The very group that preaches tolerance does not practice it. In fact, they are the most intolerant people on Earth. Liberals are the easiest callers to fluster.

I learned early on in my career to actually listen to my callers and to agree or disagree without resorting to name calling. That trait is not a liberal one.

In my talk show career, I've been cursed at, threatened with violence, even death, and harassed by liberals who cannot stand to be confronted with truth.

The typical liberal caller starts the conversation in a normal tone, but as the discussion continues they become more and more agitated, especially if confronted with facts that undercut their positions. Finally, they lose control and either curse or start name calling. That's when a host can disconnect from them. A brief pause by the host gives the audience an opportunity to see the true face of liberalism. I love those moments.

I also love the fact I had a long-time friendship with a man hated by liberals across the country. His name was Jesse Helms.

Chapter Fourteen

Senator Jesse Helms was a major target of liberals. He served in the U.S. Senate for 30 years and was a magnet for critics because he said what he meant and meant what he said. He was frequently the target of negative editorials and biased reporting by national newspapers, major networks and cable TV pundits. The newspaper of his capital city, the *News & Observer* was no exception.

At one time, I owned a radio station in Raleigh, WTRG, known as *Oldies 100.7*. I held a weekly call-in show on the station.

One day I received a call from Senator Helms thanking me for the family values and love of country I projected on my show. He was extremely kind and suggested we meet.

I was very much aware of his career and the venom directed at him by the liberal mainstream media. I was glad to have the opportunity to meet the man and judge for myself whether any of what I had heard or read about him was true or untrue.

When I met Jesse Helms I found him to be an uncommonly decent man. That first meeting began a friendship that lasted until his death.

Over the years I emceed a few fundraisers and events for Senator Helms and we had many personal discussions on a variety of topics. It was obvious he had come to trust me when he suggested we begin to record our conversations. Those talks took place in his office, his home, and occasionally my home. I believe I got to know Jesse Helms and his wife, Dot, as well as anyone outside their family.

In all of our discussions through the years, even when liberals were doing disgusting things like draping a condom look-alike over the chimney of his Washington residence, he never lost his temper or railed out against them. I found him to be a remarkable man, not the racist or homophobe he was accused of being by liberal America or the biased media.

I never heard Senator Helms utter a harsh word about people of color. He said over-and-over again that he did not hate gay people, only the sin. He had his opinions and he did not waver.

My friend, Jesse Helms, was a deeply devout Christian and prayer before a meal was mandatory. His love for his wife, Dorothy Helms, known as Dot, and his love for his family was evident.

When someone questions Helms' integrity, I can certainly respond with this fact. Think of all the powerful liberals and biased media pundits who wanted to bring him down. They moved Heaven and Earth in an attempt to find any dirt they could gather on the conservative senator.

They never succeeded. That's because he was a sincere and honorable man, one who wanted to avoid even the insinuation of impropriety. Senator Helms told me he and Dot purposely avoided all the legendary nightly parties that took place on Embassy Row and other Washington haunts. When work was done, he went home to Dot. During his 30-year span in Congress not once were his fierce critics able to pin one scandal on the man. In that city, that is an amazing feat.

Senator Helms' constituent services were the talk of the Senate. Ask anyone who ever dealt with them, and even those who did not like his beliefs and politics. They all will say his office responded to contacts for help with respect and with results. He and his staff cared and it showed.

Jesse also had several friends among Democrats. They could disagree without being disagreeable.

I'm not sure if Dot approved of our usual lunch menu when we got together for our recorded discussions. If she had not prepared a lunch at home, I would get a call from the senator.

"Tom, why don't you pick up two for you and two for me," Senator Helms would say.

He was referring to Snoopy's hot dogs. A Raleigh favorite for a long time.

"See if you can get them to put a little extra chili on mine," he would add.

I arrived for one of our lunch meetings at his home in Raleigh. Dot answered the door and led me back to Senator Helms office in his house. As she opened the door I heard Jesse talking on the phone.

"Thank you for the call, Mr. President, but I have to get off the line. My friend, Tom Joyner, just arrived with his tape recorder and we have to get to work.

It was President Bush on the phone.

I will always be grateful to Senator Helms for something he did that he was never asked to do and certainly did not have to. He sent an unsolicited letter to my daughter, son-in-law and grandchildren. It was dated March 31, 2003 and on his U.S. Senate letterhead.

Dear Bob, Lisa, Anna Marie and Neva Grace:

Please forgive me for taking the liberty of addressing you folks on a first-name basis. The fact is, I feel that I know you because a fellow named Tom Joyner and I engage in bragging contests ever so often about our respective children and grandchildren.

I am sincere in saying that Tom Joyner is one of the finest, brightest and courageous gentlemen I've ever known. There are a lot of things that I admire about Tom, but if I had to choose one of the many, it would be his unflinching honesty. He is a great American because he loves his country and respects all American principles unfailingly.

I inquired before writing this letter if he would mind my telling you about my admiration of him. He smiled and said something about my having "more important things to do."

But when it comes to your father,-father-in-law, and grandfather, I do not have anything else that could possibly be more important than telling you of my admiration of a great human being and friend.

God bless you.

Sincerely,
Jesse Helms

Needless to say, I can't tell you how much this kindness meant to me. I miss my friend every day.

In addition to a great friendship, Jesse Helms gave me valuable advice. He said I should think through my positions to make sure I am right. Then, state them forcefully. Never waiver. If you are shown to be mistaken, he said to never hesitate to acknowledge the error with an apology. However, never allow yourself to be stampeded into backing down when you know you are right.

I still have the tapes of the conversations I had with Senator Helms. He gave me permission to write a book about our experiences together. He was very candid with me and I, in return, pledged to him I would write the book but not publish it until ten years after the last to die between Jesse and his wife. I will keep that pledge.

Unfortunately, I was overseas when Jesse passed away and unable to get back in time for the funeral. At the appointed time for his funeral service, Anne and I held hands and offered up a prayer for our friend.

Chapter Fifteen

I am firm in my beliefs, and just as Jesse Helms advised me, I'm never afraid to express them. You are free to agree or disagree. That's what makes this country great. If you agree with my beliefs, I'm glad. If not, I'll borrow a line from Clark Gable in the epic movie *Gone With the Wind*: "Frankly, my dear, I don't give a damn."

I believe in God. I was baptized at the age of eight, not because I was forced to, but because I have felt the hand of God in my life as long as I can remember.

In my early childhood, when my parents would engage in drunkenness and physical attacks against one another on weekends, I found refuge in church. Like any human being I had moments that I am not proud of, but overall I have tried to live the life that I knew God wanted me to live.

I used to walk home from school and daydream. Since we had little or nothing, and my parents lacked higher education, I imagined myself becoming successful. I developed a vivid imagination and for a time I would make up stories to tell to others that were designed to make me appear better off than I was. Some were whoppers and as I look back on it today. I can see how those stories played out over time, proving not to be true and providing embarrassment.

I think there was a sense of desperation in those stories. I wanted so badly to fit in and to boost my own self esteem that I overcompensated. Thankfully, I grew out of it with the help of God.

In my early teens, I began praying that God would show me the way he wanted me to go in all that I said and all that I did. That's still a nightly prayer of mine today.

Ironically, I was petrified at the thought of speaking out before others until I got into radio. That caused me to keep my feelings about God and Christianity to myself for far too long. Today, I pray only to be a conduit for God's good works on earth. I enjoy helping others and seeing smiles on the faces of children and the elderly. I am happy to give my Christian testimony to any who care to listen.

I'm convinced it was faith in God, even at an early age, that helped me deal with many problems at home during my childhood. I mentioned my parents in the first chapter. Here are some more details.

My Father, John Thomas (JT) and my Mother, Eva Wallace Joyner never got very far in school. My dad left school in the third grade in post-depression 1930 to go to work as a gofer at an auto dealership in Wilson. My Mother got through the eighth grade in Smithfield before leaving school to assist her family.

I was conceived just after the Japanese attack on Pearl Harbor. I can only surmise that the two of them thought the end of the world was on its way and threw caution to the wind.

In total, my parents had six children, five boys and one girl. They coped during the week, worked hard and sacrificed for their children, but on weekends they sought to escape using alcohol.

I cannot overemphasis the disruption and chaos in our home, but at the same time I hasten to assure you that through it all we never stopped loving our Mother and Father or felt like they did not love us.

They began to mellow when I left to join the Navy in 1960, fresh out of Elm City High School. They had always spoke of God, but now they embraced him, accepted Jesus Christ as their Lord and Savior and found serenity for the last 30 years of their lives. I admire their courage to confront the demons inside them and to cast out the evil that had plagued them. It pains me to talk about the hard times with my parents but it is a part of my life and I don't try to pretend otherwise.

In these beginning chapters, I've hoped to share with you some of my story in hopes of you understanding how I developed my opinions on life and politics. In other words, why I believe so strongly in what I believe is right and also what

I believe is wrong in our great country known as the United States of America.

In my opinion, our representative democracy is under attack like no other time in our history. Liberals and Progressives want to, as Barack Obama said, "Fundamentally change America." Unfortunately, their idea of change can devastate all of what is great about the U.S.A.

There is a complicated list of issues before us right now that are not just ones to be concerned about, but issues that could ruin the future for our children, grandchildren and future generations. That is why I cannot remain silent.

What follows in this book is a collection of commentaries I created on those various issues. I hope and pray they will encourage those that believe as I do that they are not alone. I also strongly hope it will change the mind of those who have been indoctrinated by the Left to ascribe to ideology that threatens us.

Tom Joyner

DRAINING THE SWAMP

Chapter Sixteen

The term "draining the swamp" was used by President Trump frequently during his campaign and since his election. He is referring to the politicians and bureaucrats in Washington who have hijacked D.C. and turned its back on the people they are supposed to be serving.

We now see clearly what happens to anyone proposing to drain that fetid swamp in Washington. The vermin who created and live in that swamp become desperate and will do desperate things in order to keep the swamp infested.

Every day and every night the liberal progressives and their mainstream fake news allies spend copious amounts of time attacking President Trump and the policies that the American people elected him to follow. They are delusional and rabid in their hate. No lie is off limits, no lack of facts can stop their onslaught.

Notice that the flak is coming from all directions and is meant to undermine this President's attempts to reverse the downward spiral of America that Barack Obama and liberal progressive Democrats had us on. In the midst of this constant barrage of negativity against

Trump, the fake news media reports that Trump's approval ratings are down. Folks, it is no secret that if you dump loads manure of an otherwise clean hog it is then dishonest to report that the hog stinks.

The fake news media does not tell you that their approval ratings are far below those of Donald Trump and sinking fast. Some foaming at the mouth Democrats go so far as to say that Donald Trump is insane. By no measure is Trump insane, moreover, his actions thus far show that he is smarter than his critics.

There is a learning curve for any new President and Trump is ahead of that curve. In his haste to fulfill his promises to the American people he can't help but make mistakes. It's part of the job. What President has not made mistakes, particularly in their first few weeks in office? Barack Obama was guilty of mistakes and, unlike Donald Trump who is guiding our ship of state himself, Obama was led by the hand through the process by people like his Iranian Muslim advisor and a host of retreaded liberal Democrats. Valerie Jarrett was his Pied Piper and he marched along with the rest of the rats in Washington. Democrats keep repeating that they want to get to the bottom of their unsubstantiated claims. Getting to the bottom of things is their buzz words but there are too many Democratic Proctologists in Congress.

Speaking of getting to the bottom of things, we should demand that a Special Investigator be appointed to reopen the inquiry about the Clinton Foundation and the obstruction of justice from Hillary Clinton when she had 33,000 emails destroyed AFTER Congress had warned her against eliminating them. That's not an unproven claim, it is a fact and a clear case of Obstruction of Justice. Let's get all of the corruption, real or imagined, out in the open and let the chips fall where they may.

How can any rational person not see the connection between Hillary Clinton's loss of the Presidency and the fact that those huge donations from foreign sources to the Clinton Foundation have dried up? No more half-a-million-dollar speech offers for the glib tongue of Bill Clinton.

Was the Clinton Foundation a play for pay toy? Now that the Clinton's no longer hold power and cannot play, these foreign sources looking to curry favor with the former Secretary of State and who was believed to be a lock-in for the presidency have slinked back into the shadows and taken any future so-called donations with them. You did not see the fake news media pointing out the loss by Hillary Clinton and her billion-dollar pipeline that suddenly ran dry. That is dishonest journalism.

RACIAL STRIFE

Chapter Seventeen

As I was growing up in rural North Carolina, I spent many weekends and summers at the home of my maternal grandmother and her youngest son, Richard Wallace. We called him "Little Richard" because my Mother's sister Lola, was married to an older Richard. For reasons that I have never fully understood, "Little Richard" was black.

Family lore says that my Grandfather, A.P. Wallace was unable to conceive children because of a bad reaction to a case of the mumps and so both grandparents agreed to allow my grandmother to conceive with others. I have no idea if that is true, and I'd point out that my grandparents told "Little Richard's" brothers and sisters that his dark skin color was due to feeding him an excess of graham crackers, so their stories are suspect.

In any event, "Little Richard" was banned from public education. The segregated black school would not accept him because he denied being black and segregated white schools would not accept him because he did not appear to be white. He remained uneducated and had to rely on manual labor to survive. He and my grandmother lived on a dairy farm near Battleboro, North Carolina in a small house supplied by the diary.

I grew up hunting and fishing with "Little Richard" and while I instinctively knew that he was black, it made no difference to me. I know racism from the inside out and I've experienced it from both blacks and whites. The ease with which the label of "Racist" or "Bigot" is tossed around concerns me. Those tossing it around have never experienced racial life as I have and theirs is simply a politically correct way to attack others who hold opinions different from their own.

America In Trouble

In April 2017, a 74-year-old grandfather was shot and killed in Cleveland, Ohio as he walked home alone. The grandfather was black and the man who shot him was black. The killer selected this elderly gentleman at random, just someone to kill. He brazenly filmed the killing and posted it online for all to see. According to the shooter he had killed more than ten others and intended to kill more. Thankfully, police in Erie, Pennsylvania stopped his car there. While they attempted to arrest him, he committed suicide.

Also, in that same month, a black man in Fresno, California shot and killed three white men at random while shouting "Allah Akbar." He stated that he hated white people and considered them devils. At first, California authorities hesitated to call this a hate crime, but in the glare of publicity they finally called it what it was, a hate crime. The shooter was caught and arrested.

This leads me to the George Soros financed anarchist group Black Lives Matter. When the two shooting incidents above happened there was not a peep out of the usual race baiters, BLM, Al Sharpton, Louis Farrakhan or Jesse Jackson, to name a few. There was nothing from California Congresswoman Maxine Waters or from any black politicians who are so eager to rail out when a shooter is white. These despicable people are hypocrites and use race as a club to wield over the white population.

The 74-year-old black grandfather's life mattered. The three white men gunned down by the extremist in Fresno had lives that mattered. There was no outcry to ban guns from black people.

With three white men dead at the hands of a racist black shooter, the white community did not take to the streets rioting, looting and burning businesses. No white spokespersons rushed to the scene shouting "NO JUSTICE-NO PEACE" or inciting violence against black people. Black Lives Matter is a sham group of paid protestors whose sole job it is to divide the races. They are aided by other Soros backed anarchist groups like MoveOn.org and Media Matters.

As long as Americans; black, white, Latino or Asian; tolerate these liberal groups and individuals whose task it is to destroy America from within, they will eat away at our foundation like drunken termites. Of course, black lives matter, but no more so than the lives of any other human being. Frankly, if white people are as racist and hate filled as the race baiters claim, why do they treat black Americans better than other black Americans treat them?

Chapter Eighteen

More on Black Lives Matter

It came to light that the head honcho of Black Lives Matter is a guy named Shaun King. The Black Lives Matter group pays so called "protestors" to hold up silly, pre-printed signs, interrupt conservative speakers at public events, block busy streets and wreak as much havoc on America as possible to keep the races apart and angry.

Much of the money to pay these useful idiot anarchists comes from various far left groups formed and financed by the Socialist George Soros and other liberal billionaires.

Black Lives Matter is a slogan, not a real complaint, and their protests are not spontaneous gatherings. Many gullible black people get suckered into these so-called protests and march for free, but the leaders are handsomely paid. Most are drawing government benefits even as they protest, so they double dip. Notice that the great majority of these "protestors" are able-bodied men and women who seek confrontation rather than communication. They are free to join these protests, day or night, because they have not tied themselves down by holding a job.

Shaun King, the leader of Black Lives Matter is not black at all. His parents were both white. This man conned Oprah Winfrey out of a scholarship from her for his attendance at a historically black college. Why does it matter whether or not Shaun King is black or white? It matters because it goes to the heart of dishonesty in these organized groups.

If Louis Farrakhan can, and did, publicly call for 10,000 black men to come forward to stalk and kill white people, how can a white man operate as the head of a group called Black Lives Matter? If the call is to kill all white people should this imposter not be killed as well?

There is evil at work when people like Farrakhan and the former leader of the New Black Panther Party, Mr. Shabazz can publicly call for the killing of white people indiscriminately and not draw even a comment from Barack Obama, then Justice Department head Loretta Lynch, or self-appointed leaders of black America. That's how far we have fallen. Make no mistake, there are those among us who seek to provoke a war between the races. Such a war would be a big step in destroying our country from within.

My experience in the first 75 years of my life has been that there are many average, ordinary black Americans, as well as white Americans. We tend to get along well one-on-one, but when the anarchists groups get involved the goodwill is threatened. I don't know any people, black or white, who spend time during their day plotting against the opposite race. If you do they are people to avoid.

I'm a white male. I had no hand in that. God made that selection just as he did for those in the black community. I make no apologies for the color of my skin. I will ultimately be judged by what I did on earth, not the color of my skin, and I do not fear that judgment day. Unfortunately, there are some who choose to use skin color as a reason for hate. That is true in both the black and white communities.

The pendulum has swung from the days of slavery when blacks were oppressed by slave owners. Most American families never owned a slave, only some five percent did. Yet, all white people are made to feel guilty for the abomination of slavery. I will not accept guilt for something that happened more than 150 years ago and which did not involve me or my ancestors who never owned a slave.

The past is the past. We can remember it, as we should, but we could continue to use the past as an excuse for personal failure. My ancestors were poor farmers and carpenters. I inherited nothing from them (unless you count Gout) and the road ahead for me at birth was rocky. It was up to each of J.T. and Eva Joyner's children to sink or swim. I chose to swim. Suffice to say that if I enjoyed any "white privilege" it's news to me.

My parents were poor folks. Which privilege do rich black families enjoy?

My wife and I have just taken the first steps to help two black children in Liberia after more than 30 years of support for Mexican children through two separate organizations. These Liberian children are extremely poor and basic food supplies are difficult to obtain by their parents. We can't solve all of their problems, but we can make sure that they have food to eat and clothes to wear. We can also offer positives in their life of negatives. The main encouragement is to obtain an education. That is the key to success in Liberia as well as here in the United States.

Call me a racist if you like, because I speak the naked truth, but the God I worship knows my heart and that is the only defense I need.

Tom Joyner

HOMOSEXUALITY AND TRANSGENDER

Chapter Nineteen

When the liberal, Democrat mayor of Charlotte, Jennifer Roberts, played politics with this subject in 2016, it set the stage for pressure from the liberal community to get the citizens of North Carolina to accept what many believe is deviant behavior. Roberts led the Charlotte city fathers to pass legislation that allowed men or women to enter, at will, the bathrooms, locker rooms and showers of the opposite sex. She knew the sitting Republican governor, Pat McCrory, would oppose that legislation and that would put him in the headlines during a reelection campaign.

Democrats were desperate to put one of their own, Roy Cooper, into the statehouse and this was a divisive issue that was sure to hurt the Republican. The Republican majority in the House and Senate passed House Bill 2 (HB2) to block the invasion of privacy. Sure enough, groups like the NCAA banned tournaments and events in the state at a cost to North Carolina of hundreds of millions of dollars.

Liberals across America were up in arms, demanding that the state rescind HB2. They spoke only about allowing transgender people to enter rest rooms. They downplayed the invasion of locker rooms and showers, something that outraged conservatives.

It was well known that transgender people had been entering bathrooms of the opposite sex based not on their sex but on what they imagined their sex to be and no one had raised a fuss about it because the transgender people did not make an issue of their presence. They went into stalls, away from prying eyes, and left when the call of nature had been answered.

That was not enough for the liberals, they wanted to publicize the event and demand that everyone accept what many found unacceptable. They had gotten legislation on the books that would allow grown men to enter the locker rooms and showers of women and girls.

For my part, I consider homosexuals, lesbians and transgendered people to be accountable only to the God who made them. I draw the line when being forced to endorse the lifestyle. I remember my friend, Jesse Helms, speaking often about how we can hate the sin and yet love the sinner.

I have several friends who are gay, but none who are flamboyant around me or who seek a spotlight. No one should be discriminated against, but we have to realize that what some consider discrimination, others consider common sense. Is a woman or child not discriminated against if subjected to a nude man in their locker room or shower? Do they not deserve privacy?

I watched with interest on April 21, 2017 as Diane Sawyer interviewed Caitlyn Jenner, formerly known as Bruce. It did help me better understand the plight of transgendered people. I have no animosity towards them and certainly no hate. I'm fully prepared to accept their right to be whoever they want to be, but opening locker rooms and showers that take away the privacy of one gender to compensate for a more confused gender is not the way to go.

Have unisex bathrooms, locker rooms and showers and I drop my argument. However, as long as a law is on the books that allows men into my granddaughter's private dressing and shower areas I will fight it. One woman on Sawyer's show said that her daughter had seen her son naked and she had no problem with it. Sawyer did not ask the follow up question: Will you also have no problem with it if a 55-year-old man watches your daughter naked? That's the danger of allowing nonsensical laws.

If you are gay or transgender I have no bone to pick with you and would defend you against bullying, but don't insist that I endorse your lifestyle. You don't need my endorsement and I will not give it.

Tom Joyner

IMMIGRATION

Chapter Twenty

I smile when I hear liberals say that we have a nation built by immigrants. While it is true that immigrants contributed much to the building of America they were LEGAL immigrants. They cried with joy as their ship passed the Statue of Liberty on its way to Ellis Island. They did not cry "discrimination" when checked for diseases or when asked what they planned to do in America. They couldn't wait to learn the English language and assimilate into our culture.

Many arrived with only the shirt on their back and a few dollars in their pockets and they did not head first to a welfare office or a government handout. Instead, they immediately set out to find employment. Most of them had talents that they could contribute to the growth of America, whether as a tailor, a plumber or other fields of expertise. Contrast that to today when immigrants, legal and illegal, come here expecting to take advantage of the government safety net strung up by liberal Democrats.

With the election of Donald Trump the influx of illegal aliens crossing our border with Mexico has decreased drastically. The word spread around Mexico and Central America that Barack Obama was soft on illegal border crossings into America, now the word has gone out that this Trump guy isn't fooling around and will no longer allow catch and release. Now, it's catch and deport. And if you come back looking a sanctuary city to hide in, run by naïve liberal Democrats, border patrol agents will be on you like Bill Clinton on an intern.

America is still the land of opportunity; but with that opportunity comes personal responsibility. Hard work and honesty opens doors in America. Laziness closes doors. While liberals in this country gripe and moan about their country those who arrive here legally find us to be the last frontier of freedom in the world.

I have a friend who came to America from Viet Nam with her husband and children. It took her almost ten years to get legal clearance to come to the United States and cost her almost $20,000. She runs a nail salon and works 70-80 hours a week. She and her family are grateful to have had an opportunity to become citizens in our country. They love America and say so at every opportunity.

This is a family that knows what hardship really is and the whole family quickly mastered English and joined a Christian church. Their children excel in school and are well-behaved. Why is it fair for this lady and her family to watch immigrants jump to the front of the line or avoid the line all together? She paid her dues and contributes to the fabric of America. I've been to Viet Nam and talked with people like this lady and I've seen firsthand the suffering of Vietnamese peasants. We don't owe them or anyone else a free ride in America, but we should welcome those who come here, as this lady's family did, to contribute to and not take away from our country.

I find it ironic that the bleeding hearts in America can't see that it is not the responsibility of western countries to take in the world's huddled masses. The days when we could afford to take more of them in are over. The government safety net designed by liberal Democrats has been terribly abused. While progressives and countries in our world who won't allow these refugees in chastise the United States for trying to protect the security of its people, Muslim countries refuse to take any of the horde of migrating Muslims into their midst. They know the danger.

Saudi Arabia is the poster child for denial of Muslim refugees. The Saudis have more than one million (closer to two million) luxurious tents with air conditioning sitting unused, but refuse to allow a single Muslim refugee into that housing. Iran is just as hypocritical in its dealings with Syrian refugees.

The bottom line is that the United States cannot, and should not, try to burden our taxpayers with some bogus duty owed to Muslim refugees. Of course, not all of these refugees are a danger to us, but, again, how do we know which ones plan to shout Allah Akbar on our streets while killing non-believers? If their own Muslim brothers are afraid to take them in why should the burden fall on America?

Chapter Twenty-One

The Cost of Illegal Immigration

At the federal level, only about one-third of this financial burden is matched by tax collections from illegal aliens. At the state and local level, an average of less than five percent of the public costs associated with illegal immigration is recouped through taxes collected from illegal aliens. Most illegal aliens do not pay any income taxes. Among those who do much of the revenues collected are refunded to the illegal aliens when they file tax returns.

With many state budgets in deficit, policymakers have an obligation to look for ways to reduce the fiscal burden of illegal immigration. California, facing a budget deficit of $14.4 billion dollars from 2010 to 2011, is hit with an estimated $21.8 billion dollars in annual expenditures on illegal aliens. Still, the aim of their far-left Governor, Jerry "Moonbeam" Brown is to invite more illegal immigration into that state. He is adamant that California become a sanctuary state where illegal aliens can hide from detection, even those with criminal records with multiple deportations.

Extreme liberalism is not confined to Hollywood. New York's $6.8 billion deficit is smaller than its $9.5 billion dollar yearly cost for illegal aliens. Both California and New York are led by extreme liberals. Both states may soon seek a bailout from taxpayers.

What is the cost to each of us as taxpayers to support 30 million illegal aliens, many of whom are working in the underground economy and not contributing to the tax system? It is estimated that the annual gross cost to U.S. taxpayers to provide schooling, medical care, and other benefits for the estimated 30 million illegal aliens is $400 billion dollars per year and rapidly increasing. Yet, they are using the system that bona fide taxpayers provide and pay for.

Illegal aliens, on average, tend to have larger families than citizens in the United States. This difference puts a strain on the resources of school districts in particular. The arrival of illegal immigrants creates a problem that is often under the radar: a black market for goods and services. Black markets are not regulated or taxed by federal or state government which means that the goods and services traded there do not contribute to the tax base. This influx of lower income, less-educated illegal aliens drives down the wages of ordinary Americans. Illegal aliens have a history of working for extremely low wages and the minimum wage of the United States is a windfall for them. However, when they take that low wage job it puts an American worker out of work.

Illegal aliens also drive up insurance rates. Drivers in many states pay a higher amount for car insurance because they are surrounded by more uninsured motorists. Going back to 2010, the average unlawful immigrant household received around $24,721 dollars in government benefits and services while paying some $10,334 in taxes. This generated an average annual deficit of around $14,387 dollars per household. That cost has to be borne by American taxpayers. Under current law, all unlawful immigrant households together have an aggregate annual deficit of around $54.5 million dollars. Are you beginning to see why a wall on our southern border to stop this illegal immigration is not only a good idea but would cost little or nothing after these annual deficit costs are subtracted?

Some people argue that illegal immigrants do work that the Americans won't do. The fact is that illegal aliens do work that Americans can't do because Americans must adhere to minimum wage and labor laws. Illegals obviously don't have to obey those laws. This is the 21st century equivalent to slavery. When it pays more to be on welfare than to work at jobs like chamber maids or apple pickers, Americans prefer welfare. Illegal immigrants have no choice.

When cheap labor dominates the market, overall wages go down. When wages go down

American workers are harmed and when
American workers are harmed it is always the
poor who feel the first hit. In a free market
helping illegal families invariably harms legal
families.

Chapter Twenty-Two

The Shadow Side of Immigration

There is a shadow side to the population that needs to be considered. U.S. immigration policy has, with a wink and a nod, encouraged the growth of a low-rate sector that is supplied to a large degree by unauthorized workers. In that regard, perhaps employers and consumers benefit, but as citizens we are abetting the growth of an underprivileged class and as taxpayers we are subsidizing employers.

According to the best estimate, 17 percent of those in federal prison are illegal aliens and they run up a substantial cost. More than $60 billion dollars is earned by illegal workers in the United States each year and is one of Mexico's largest revenue streams. After exports and oil sales, this is money sent home by legal immigrants and illegal aliens working in the United States. This is a massive transfer of wealth from America, essentially from America's displaced working poor to Mexico.

There is far more that I could detail for you, but after a while all of these numbers seem to run together. Politically, we stand today at a crossroads. We can take the road to cooperation, common sense and patriotism or we can take the road to petty politics, obstructionism and party before country.

Chapter Twenty-Three

Sanctuary Cities

To demonstrate how far America has fallen, we need only look at liberal controlled areas that have been designated as sanctuary cities. Some liberal Governors want to declare entire states as sanctuary havens. Our founding Father's would roll over in their graves at the idea of providing a safe haven for criminals.

Those who enter the United States illegally are criminals. The very act of breaking the law is a criminal activity. Sanctuary cities, like San Francisco, welcome illegal aliens and help them hide from detection by security officers. Many of these illegal immigrants have been deported several times and some are drug dealers, rapists and killers. The left likes to say that human beings are not illegal. True, but their activities are illegal.

President Trump threatens to stop federal aid flowing into sanctuary cities unless they stop illegal aliens from hiding from the authorities with the city's blessings. Predictably, liberal America is outraged. Just as they demand the admittance of Syrian refugees who cannot be fully vetted, they seek to hide illegal aliens from deportation. California's Governor Jerry "Moonbeam" Brown, Chicago's loopy Mayor Rahm Emmanuel and New York City's racist Mayor Bill DeBlasio are champions of sanctuary cities and states. Each was elected to office with promises of more free stuff.

California is on the brink of bankruptcy and boasts the largest contingent of liberal loony birds in the United States, all housed in and around Hollywood. These people are hypocrites who direct you to do as they say, not as they do. Who else fly's a private jet to an energy saving conference? Who else would vote a straight Democratic ticket when the party is led by people like Barack Obama, Hillary Clinton, Nancy Pelosi, Harry Reid (retired, thank God), Chuckie Shumer, Elijah Cummings, Maxine Waters, Elizabeth "I be an injun" Warren, Debbi Wasserman-Schultz (fired by the Democratic National Committe for underhanded politics and immediately hired by Hillary Clinton) and Bernie "Comrade" Sanders to name just a few.

But, I digress. Anybody endorsing sanctuary cities, a safe hiding place for criminals, is at best ignorant or at worst willing to sacrifice our security.

Chapter Twenty-Four

On immigration, left-wingers pretty much support open borders. They support people from other countries coming to America and receiving all of the government aid available to them. The more the merrier. In the future, it is a fact that Caucasians will be in the minority in America. There is a flood of immigrants coming in from Mexico and Latin America and the black population is expanding. What will that mean?

To understand the future let's look at some facts within the white, black and Latino communities, like education scores, crime rates, unemployment rates, poverty rates; and rank each race from first to third with first being the best and third being the worst.

The facts show that the white race is first, Latinos are ranked second and blacks are ranked third. That's not a judgment on individuals, just facts on the categories that I mention for ratings. These statistics also correlate to how well the countries represented by these races are doing.

First, look at the countries that are primarily white, like America, Canada and European countries. They are typically prosperous with lower unemployment and poverty rates. Next, let's look at the countries that are primarily

Latino. Latin American countries are on the poorer side with higher unemployment and poverty rates.

Finally, look at the countries that are primarily black, like those in Africa. Despite the fact many of those countries have valuable resources, they are basically undeveloped, poor, with horrible unemployment and poverty rates. This is not about individuals, many of whom are decent people, but who lack the power to force out their despotic leaders. It is about the countries and communities they build and live in. I realize that saying things that are true, but that others may not want to hear, opens one up to charges of being a racist or bigot. I am neither, I am a realist.

It's pretty much a fact that if things keep going the way they are the Democrat party will become the ruling party in American politics because approximately 90% of blacks and 65-70% of Latinos vote democratic.

Current Democrat policies include their opposition to controlling our borders and their insistence on the protections they offer to illegal aliens entering our country, including declaring sanctuary cities that shelter these illegal aliens from detection. These sanctuary cities allow illegal aliens who are caught and deported to return and be protected, even those who have committed crimes in this country.

If they are allowed to prevail, America will become a Socialist country. They will massively redistribute wealth by raising taxes to punish achievers and offer free rides to the unproductive among us. Like socialist countries before us, we will collapse.

When efforts are suggested to reduce taxes on corporations, the people who provide the jobs and are taxed at the world's highest rate, Democrats resort to their age-old mantra about tax cuts for the rich. Ironically, the main career Democrats are among the richest, but have clever lawyers and CPAs to lower their own taxes.

We need jobs in this country and poor people cannot supply those jobs. If we continue to tax our job producers at rates that make it harder for them to keep jobs in America and compete on the world market, the needed jobs will not materialize.

Socialism may be able to last in America for a while because we have a strong upper class and the government will be able to milk money from the rich until all go broke.

We need money to buy or rent a house, a car, to buy food and all the basic necessities. We get that by working. When we give people free money, free food, subsidized rent, cell phones and other goodies, we should not be surprised when many cut down their working hours or stop working all together. In addition, all of this free stuff being doled out, at the expense of the approximately 50% of us who pay taxes, attracts more people outside of America for all the wrong reasons.

There is still time...though time is short...to stop the stampede of liberalism in our country. All it takes for us to lose our freedom and liberty is for the average, ordinary American to give up. That's what our enemies, inside and outside of our borders, are counting on.

We must open our minds and forget the past. Seek out truth because, given the bias and fake news from the liberal mainstream media, truth will be elusive. Don't accept information at face value without looking at who and where that information comes from. Our greatest military might cannot save us if we are not willing to save ourselves. Some say that ignorance is bliss but I disagree. Ignorance is ignorance and if we remain in a state of ignorance we deserve what will ultimately happen to us.

Chapter Twenty-Five

The Cost of Immigration

We hear so much, pro and con, about immigration into America. So, what are the real facts and the truth?

First, let's concede that the wall that President Trump will build between the United States and Mexico will not be cheap. Estimates range from a low of $12 billion to as much as $22 billion.

Many on the left and in the liberal fake news media point to the cost of the wall with fake outrage, but they fail to point out the cost of illegal immigration. When that cost is subtracted from the cost of building the wall the American taxpayer is the winner.

Illegal immigration costs U.S. taxpayers about $113 billion dollars a year at the Federal, State and local levels. Education for the children of illegal aliens constitutes the single largest cost to taxpayers with an annual price tag of nearly $52 billion dollars a year.

If not for that burden from illegal immigration the wall could be built three times;

and remember, those costs of illegal immigration are not a one-time expense as the wall will be, but yearly expenditures.

Radical Islam

Chapter Twenty-Six

Religion of Peace?

As more and more Muslim terrorists kill and maim across the world in the name of Islam we continue to be told that Islam is a religion of peace. I'll share some facts later in this book which question the claim of peaceful Islam.

Followers of Islam love to tell us that not all Muslims are terrorists That's true but it's also true that almost all terrorists are Muslims. The problem is that we cannot tell the difference between a Muslim terrorist and one professing peace. Not all snakes are venomous either, but it only takes one to kill us.

The history of Islam shows it in constant war for more than 1,400 years. Its founder, Mohammed, proclaimed himself a prophet and set about to dominate the world. The bible of Islam, the Quran makes it clear that Islam and Christianity cannot possibly co-exist. Muslims who try to leave the faith are to be killed, according to the Quran, and anyone who does not believe in Islam must be killed by followers of

Islam. Women are as low as cattle in Islam. Men totally dominate the faith.

The stated aim of Islam is to dominate the world, eradicating all who do not share the belief. Looking back in history, we see a distinctive pattern among Muslims. They migrate into a country such as Great Britain and live quietly for years. It is only when they gain enough followers that they start making demands on the host country. We see that in Europe today, especially in London, where Muslims demand that Sharia law replace British laws.

Muslims concentrate their population in a particular area and then make it a fortress by denying entry to the police. They have no intention of adopting the customs and values of the host country. They will not assimilate, but insist on the host country changing its customs and values to match what they left behind in their home country. That begs the question of why they migrate to another country that does not share their customs and values when they know full well that they are guests.

The answer is simple. They cannot stay in their home country and dominate the world as they are called to do by the Quran. It is necessary to spread out across the globe, grow in population, and then agitate for the changes they seek. I am a Christian and my God does not command me to kill those of other faiths. In fact, one of the Ten Commandments given to Moses

specifically states that THOU SHALT NOT
KILL. If I choose to leave the Christian faith I do
so without fear that another Christian will seek
me out and kill me. Those are reasons, among
others, why Islam and Christianity will never be
compatible.

Our Christian God does not send us out to
harm Muslims. They should not be discriminated
against or persecuted, but we should keep a
wary eye on a people who are instructed by their
bible to lie to non-believers in order to advance
Islam. I believe that it is up to the Muslims
among us, who are not practicing violence
against us, to become more vocal against what
they say is the perversion on their religion. How
can you say that the Islamic terrorists have
hijacked your religion and not do all in your
power to help reclaim it? The radicals are known
in the neighborhood and yet it is rare that they
are reported by their Islamic neighbors. That has
to change.

Chapter Twenty-Seven

Islam and America. Compatible?

Abd Al-Karim Bakkar is a Syrian academic who first said, in 2009, that democracy and Islam are not, and cannot be compatible. He said that democracy runs counter to Islam on several issues: In a democracy legislation it is the prerogative of the people. It is the people who draw up the constitution, and they have the authority to amend it as well.

Islam differs; this is self-evident in the fact that Islamic theocracy rules throughout the Islamic world, crushing human rights such as those delineated in our Bill of Rights. In some secular states like Turkey and Egypt, democracy is tolerated only to gain acceptance from the west. However, try telling a Coptic Christian in Egypt, for example, about freedom of religion or try imposing a government dictate contrary to Islam.

Under Islam and Sharia law there is no freedom of religion or speech and equal rights are forbidden to women and non-Muslims. If you convert from Islam to Christianity you have signed your death warrant.

Tunisian Author Saleem Ben Ammar wrote this: "To hell with democracy, long live Islam!"

One hundred percent of Muslims agree with what he said. To say anything else is apostacy from Islam. These two competing political systems are diametrically opposed to each other. You can't be democratic and be a Muslim, or a Muslim and be democratic.

It is a fact that a President of the United States, regardless of their political party affiliation, cannot uphold, defend and support the Constitution of the United States and adhere to Sharia law. It cannot be done because Sharia says NO. It's not the Constitution of the United States that must govern. It is Sharia law.

A report from the Center for Security Policy documented the threat posed by Islam and Sharia law to our democracy, our government, our constitution, and our way of life. The report concludes that the Sharia is "totalitarian" and incompatible with the U.S. Constitution, our system of democratic law making and the constitutional guarantees of freedom of conscience, individual liberty and freedom of expression, including the right to criticize Sharia law itself.

The report further cites a document from the Muslim Brotherhood on North America describing a covert process of Islamic settlement in the United States. The plan is to carry out a grand Jihad in eliminating and destroying western civilization from within and "sabotaging its miserable house by our hands and the hands of believers so that it is eliminated."

These documents and statements by Muslim clerics and radical Islamists are warnings of their intentions that we would be foolish to ignore. We ignored the announced goals of Adolph Hitler in his book, *Mein Kampf*, which brought us a horrific war and the murder of six million Jews.

Sharia is used around the world to condone barbarities such as the stoning and subjugation of women and the execution of homosexuals. It does not support freedom of speech, conscience or religion, or even equal treatment under the law.

This is the same Muslim Brotherhood that was endorsed by Barack Obama and the same Muslim Brotherhood from whom Obama selected operatives to come into our government in sensitive security areas. Obama's Muslim enforcer, Valerie Jarrett, is a hard-core believer in Islam and her influence on Obama was evident.

Barack Obama said that if the political winds shifted, he would side with Islam, not America. He also said that the future must not belong to those who threaten Islam. What he should have said is that the future must not belong to those who threaten the U.S. constitution, and that is at the core of Islamic Sharia law.

Amid several global crises that we face today, the debate on the nature of Islam, vis a' vie security, refugees, and even economic policy, has created the biggest controversy. The fake news media has featured a series of opinion pieces written by educated, liberal thinkers that claim to dispel myths about Sharia law being against western values. One in the Washington Post claimed that Sharia is in favor of everything ranging from a western-style government to gender equality. Another piece by the Huffington Post claimed that the definition of Jihad refers primarily to sustained effort advancing the common good and reprimanding evil.

The reality could not be further from these ideas, which are based upon reinterpretations of vague verses from the Quran. The most common argument made in favor of a progressive Islam is that the Quran and other scriptures can be subject to interpretation. That's an argument than confuses observation with suggestion. The argument implies that the Quran's commandments change, depending on where and when it is being read. So, whereas the punishment for sedition is death in Islam, simply because of the fact that it is being read in a different time period, in a different place, the punishment no longer applies. However, if the Quran changes depending on whose reading it, then the Quran itself does not have any commandments.

For any devout Muslim, believing that Allah does not really command anything is a major problem. It is fundamental in Islam that the revelations from the Quran are to be applied after contextualizing through Hadith in order to reach an objective and time honored verdict.

Some go so far as to claim that in true Islam, politics and religion would not even be combined into a single force. That is ironic considering that the Islamic state under Prophet Mohammed, and under his companions for CE 622 to 661, did exactly that. In fact, it is impossible within that period to find a single time period for which a religious law was not enforced by the state.

Others have noted that countries like Saudi Arabia, Iran and Pakistan are not true Islamic countries applying Sharia, pointing out that colonialism is primarily to blame for the policies of those countries. That's true, however it is also fact that a truly Islamic country would have much of the same laws that are decried by the west. They include beheadings, cutting of hands for stealing, and criminalization of homosexuality and adultery. If anything, it is the colonial remnants of Muslim countries that keep them from applying Sharia law.

There are two primary meanings of the word Jihad. Anybody who has read the saying of the Prophet Mohammed will appreciate that every single time the word Jihad is used by a Hadith, it is reference to war. It is argued that the Quranic verse stating that: "There shall be no compulsion in religion," found in Chapter 2, verse 256, affirms freedom of religion. But that does not mean freedom of religion as understood in the west.

Under a truly Islamic regime people are allowed to believe and practice in the faith they want to. However, non-Muslims in an Islamic state are not given the same privileges as Muslims. For example, non-Muslims pay separate and higher taxes. Even in the criminal code a Muslim that kills a non-Muslim cannot be given the death penalty. So, even if religion is not coerced it is a fact that having a different faith means being treated differently in an Islamic state, contrary to the western notion that religions should not affect rights and responsibilities as a citizen. Furthermore, changing one's religion from Islam to another religion warrants the death penalty.

It is popularly argued that because Sharia is considered progressive and feminist in the time it was created in the 7th century CE, it is therefore in favor of a progressive agenda that is prevalent today. That is far from the truth. Reinterpretation to favor trimester abortion, changing divorce laws favoring men, or even laws restricting women from leaving the house without their husband's permission are all laws that are part of Islam. Ignoring Islamic scripture does not make it go away. The simple fact is that Islam and democracy, as we know it, are not compatible and never will be.

Chapter Twenty-Eight

What is C.A.I.R.?

What do you know about C.A.I.R, the Council on American-Islamic relations?

C.A.I.R was created by the Muslim Brotherhood, an Islamic supremacist organization that pioneered 20th century Islamic terrorism and sanctions violence against civilians. The truth is that C.A.I.R has only about 5000 members, even though the membership fee is just ten dollars. They represent the opinions of only 12% of Muslim-Americans according to Gallup.

C.A.I.R receives financial support from foreign powers who have also provided direct support to Osama Bin Laden, Al-Qaeda and Hamas. The organization has solicited money from sponsors of terror and received financial support from convicted terrorists.

C.A.I.R founders have praised terrorists to Muslim audiences and said that suicide bombers are acting on behalf of Islam. C.A.I.R also raised funds for terrorists under the guise of helping 9-

11 victims. Their members have called for the overthrow of the United States and the imposition of Sharia law. C.A.I.R has also suggested applying Sharia punishment of death to users who criticize Islam on the Internet.

There's more: At least 15 high level C.A.I.R staff members have been under federal investigation for ties to Islamic terrorism. They have discouraged Muslim-Americans from cooperating with law enforcement and have spent more time and money advocating on behalf of convicted terrorists than for Islam. It was C.A.I.R that tweeted that American sniper Chris Kyle was a hate-filled killer and that those of us who consider him a hero are simplistic patriots.

C.A.I.R gets far more media attention than they deserve. Here is what their Vice-Chairman, Sarwat Husain, said about the media in this country: "Media in the United States is very gullible and they will see that if you have something, especially as a Muslim. If you have something to say they will come running to you. Take advantage of that."

Does anyone really believe that if the Muslim population were to become the majority in America, Christians would be able to live in peace? This is the great deception of some on the left and right.

Why is it that only a handful of Christian refugees were admitted to America during the Obama administration? Middle Eastern

Christians are the ones being specifically targeted and killed.

In May 2017, ISIS took responsibility for dressing in government uniforms and stopping a bus in Egypt. Once stopped, the bus was sprayed with bullets and occupants were led into the desert where they were brutally slaughtered. Those occupants were Coptic Christians. But, while the Christians in the Middle East are being persecuted, the left is dumping immigrants into America without any regard to the fact that those already here, by and large, do not want to assimilate into American culture.

We should allow no one else into this country who does not come here to assimilate and embrace our system and values. Not just Muslims, anyone. We have no obligation to take in the world's problems. Other countries, including Mexico, have serious laws that prevent people from coming there to stay who would be a drain on their economy. If you wish to live in Mexico for instance, you have to demonstrate that you have enough resources to support yourself. By contrast, the left in America pushes us to offer more cash and benefits to immigrants, legal or illegal.

C.A.I.R has been listed as a terrorist organization by the United Arab Emirates and has, as its mission, to character anyone or organization critical of Islam and Islamic extremism as either promoting hatred of Muslims or supporting anti-Islam themes.

C.A.I.R. and has been active in shutting down free speech in the name of Islamaphobia.

It is important for Americans to know and understand what C.A.I.R is what its motives are. They are connected to Hamas, which the United States has designated as a terrorist organization. It's the same terrorist organization that pays a bounty to Palestinians who kill Israelis. The head of C.A.I.R, Nighad Awad, publicly declared his support for Hamas. The Holy Land Foundation, a Hamas front group, donated five thousand dollars to Hamas, and, in turn, C.A.I.R exploited the 9-11 attacks to raise money for the Holy Land Foundation.

Demonstrators at a C.A.I.R sponsored rally in Florida chanted "We are Hamas. Average Americans don't have the time to delve into these subjects of my weekly Commentarys, but they do want to be informed about dangers confronting us. C.A.I.R is one of those organizations that is dangerous.

When we allow such organizations to label us guilty of Islamophobia in order to take our attention off of the dangers of Islamic extremism we do so at our peril. C.A.I.R is active in shutting down the speech of anyone it has labeled anti-Muslim. They were successful in getting an FBI representative to withdraw from speaking at a Texas event called Domestic Jihad and ISIS, hosted by St Mary's University Center for terrorism law in San Antonio.

They then called on Oklahoma Senator Kyle Loveless to drop a bill that states that school districts would incur no liability as a result of providing an elective course in the objective study of religion and the Bible. It was to have been an elective course, and no one would have been commanded to attend, but C.A.I.R wants no speech allowed which might, in any way, expose Islamic extremism.

The term Islamophobia is itself misleading. Is not Islamophobia to fear Jihad? While it is true that the majority of Muslims in America do not support Islamic extremism, it is also true that many Muslims do, and many of them agitate, for Sharia law to be established in America. We have every right to be concerned and afraid of that possibility.

I do not, and I don't believe that most Americans do, have a problem with Muslims or their devotion to Islam. The Christian God we follow does not command us to kill non-believers. What I do have is the stated aim of Islam to dominate the world, to subjugate all of us to Islam.

Most Americans have never read the Quran, the Bible of Islam. Followers are told, and they believe, that every word of the Quran is the direct word of Allah. If one believes that then it is not possible to avoid the passages in the Quran that demand the killing of Infidels, non-believers. There are many passages in the Quran that rational people can disagree with and yet

Islam's followers demand blind obedience for themselves and for non-believers.

Every American should educate themselves about movements and individuals who seek to separate us from our Christian God. We need not discriminate against those who follow Islam, but we must be vigilant against those who see Islam as the only way and seek to dominate the world in the name of Allah.

Chapter Twenty-Nine

In May of 2017, Islamic terrorists killed 22 innocent people in Manchester, England, while they were attending a pop concert. The main attacker had recently returned from Libya, one of the countries President Trump called for immigration to be suspended from until we can properly vet them.

This suicide bomber's two brothers, and his father and several others, were arrested. The brother confessed to being prepared to carry out his own suicide bombing. ISIS has claimed responsibility for this carnage and that makes them mass murderers.

Any country on earth who will not cooperate in eliminating these savages from our world is as responsible for these terrorist attacks as ISIS is.

Great Britain brought much of this terror upon itself by allowing mass migration of people from countries where Islamic terrorism is applauded and where many of the terrorists are allowed to train.

It is time for the world to unite behind the effort to rid the world of radical Islam. Any country that harbors Islamic extremists, allows them to train there, or in any way refuses to take real action against them, should be a pariah throughout the world. Cut off aid, freeze their bank accounts, and do the same to any country that supports these pariahs. It is simply a matter of time before those bombings increase in America.

We allow unfettered travel between many countries throughout the world, especially those that are supposed to be our friends. But, those countries allow these Islamic terrorists to travel to countries like Libya, Afghanistan, Syria and others, and then return. That's how the Manchester bomber was able to carry out his deadly mission.

This madman was born in Great Britain. He was a second-generation Islamic follower. There are a great many of them in our own country. We either stop Islamic terrorism now or allow it to engulf us. Liberal Democrats will never allow President Trump to take the measures necessary to stop it. To do so would be to admit that Trump is right. So, these dastardly political animals are willing to risk our lives for their greed and power.

Liberal judges in our country continue to block Trump's travel ban which allows the Islamic terrorists to get into America and wait their turn to kill and maim. When the next great massacre happens here in America, and it will, these judges and liberal Democrats will have that blood on their hands. Pray that your children and grandchildren are not among those innocents slaughtered, as in Manchester.

r">
115

Time for a Humor Break
Y'all, Meet Clyde Rambo

Chapter Thirty

Several years ago, when I owned Oldies 100.7 and did my weekly talk show that caught the attention of Senator Jesse Helms, I created an alter ego I named Clyde Rambo. Clyde was as country as a corn cob and spoke his mind. While Clyde made lots of people laugh, he became the epitome of the saying, "In all good humor, there is a little bit of truth."

Here is some of Clyde's wisdom:

"I don't like to go to New York. I find the people there to be surly and somebody always has a hand out for a tip, even when they ain't done nothin.' They can separate you from your dinero faster than Colonel Sanders can pluck a chicken. I know there's some good folks in New York, I just never met 'em.

"And the little woman? That's her right there on the couch. We used to go up there at Christmas time to look in the pretty windows, but we stopped that when an Ethiopian cab driver took us on a suicide run through Chinatown. He wanted to be paid for it, with a tip!"

"Some people say New York folks can't get along, but that ain't true. I saw two New Yorkers sharin' a cab. One of 'em took the tires and the other one took the engine."

"Somebody asked me the other day how it feels to be married so long. I said it felt wonderful cause I never did like that dating stuff no way. At least in my day you felt good holdin' the door for a lady. Today, that lady might cuss you out and kick your cat.

"Leonard Wiley asked me how he was supposed to get married. He said, 'Every woman I bring home, my Ma don't like.'

"I said, 'Leonard, all you have to do is find somebody who's just like your mama.'

Leonard said he'd done that already. That was the one his daddy didn't like."

"Speakin' of winning the lottery, Sally Hudson hit it big and decided to treat herself to a milk bath. Sally called the milk man and told him to bring her 96 quarts of milk the next day. The milk man said he'd do that and then asked her, 'Mrs. Hudson, do you want that milk pasteurized?' Sally thought for a minute and then said, 'Nah, just up to my chest will do it.'

"The fast food folks are under pressure to pay $15.00 an hour to folks behind the counter who can't put two burgers into a sack without GPS.

"Ronald McDonald is not the real clown these misfits think he is. There will be robots where they used to stand when we come in for the next Big Mac.

"Some folks is too dumb to light a candle and they think that somebody is gonna pay them $15.00 an hour to take up space. So, bring on them robots. We'll just punch in our order and actually get what we paid for.

"The robots won't pick their nose or screw up our change. Just might work."

"Have y'all ever wondered why it has been the best time to buy a care for the last 30 years? This guy on TV told me 30 years ago that I had to hurry in because I might not get this opportunity again. Thirty years later, I'm hearin' that offer is still open. I ain't sure how this works, but if that 1986 jalopy I rushed in to buy in 1986 ever stops runnin', it is sure good to know that it will still be the best time to buy a car. Anybody else confused?"

"Birds are born with wings, and at some point they are expected to fly out on their own, and they do.

"Compare that to young folks today that expect Ma and Pa to keep them in the nest, feed 'em, clothe 'em and make their college give them a safe place where they can gather and snivel.

"Course they also want to be free to protest where the rest of us have our safe place.

"It's got so bad that even if they move away they circle around and come back like a boomerang in the outback.

"We got to tell them that if they have all the social answers on campus then it's time to question why they can't buy their own jockey shorts and feed their own face."

"Some of us is old enough to remember outhouses. Kids today think an outhouse is where you go when you're tagged out at second base. But, we know better.

"The thang sat back about 50 yards from the house and aroma was the only GPS you needed to find it.

"Back then, I had a brother-in-law who couldn't sleep cause he drunk so much beer during the day and had to follow that little path out back a lot.

"It won't so bad in the summer time, and spring and fall was tolerable; but, when winter come along, that old boy gave new meaning to 'dashing through the snow.'"

"Hollywood liberals are a hoot. Take that Barbara Streisand. She thought that Obama hung the Moon rather than flushing it down the toilet.

"Barbara has been around for a while. She has more crows' feet that that tribe in Wyoming. I ain't saying she's long in the tooth, but Buzzy Sharpe says she is older than the sandals Moses wore to sic them frogs and locusts on the pharaoh."

Clyde Rambo retired a few years ago, but those who question his wisdom "ain't" very smart.

I hope you enjoyed some comments from Clyde. Now, let's get serious again about what is happening in our country.

Tom Joyner

Liberals, Fox News & Fake News

Chapter Thirty-One

Bill O'Reilly held down the number one cable news show on Fox News for 16 years. His was an extremely powerful voice which tended to be more conservative than liberal and that set him up for constant attacks by the liberal mainstream media and a Democrat party filled with hypocrites.

Fox News is owned by Rupert Murdock, but Murdock is quite elderly now and his two sons have moved into positions of power at Fox. Both are extremely liberal and were happy to find chinks in O'Reilly's armor. Still, O'Reilly's programs brought hundreds of millions of dollars into the Fox coffers each year and that made him valuable to the network. That was the point of attack from liberal Democrats and their mainstream media flunkies.

A group of women suddenly appeared behind the far-left Democrat attorney Gloria Allred to claim that O'Reilly had made suggestive remarks to them years ago. No one suggested that he was guilty of placing hands upon them or assaulting them in any way, as had been the case with Bill Clinton while president. At the time, these same hypocritical Democrats rallied around Clinton, who had been impeached for lying under oath, to save him. They ignored the claims of assaults and rape from women who came forward. These same hypocritical people now sought the assassination of Bill O'Reilly for far less.

It wasn't just Clinton the liberals circled the wagons for. When Ted Kennedy drove his car off a Massachusetts pier in the middle of the night, with a young woman in that car, and swam away leaving her to die, fellow Democrats became eerily silent. The "Lion of the Senate" was married. So much for concern about abused women by hypocritical Democrats.

The anarchists organized a boycott of O'Reilly's sponsors, including coercion financed by billionaire George Soros. Sponsors were intimidated and withdrew from the program.

Feeling emboldened, these fanatics seized upon a comment made by Fox correspondent, Jesse Waters about Ivanka Trump. They insinuated that Waters had made a lewd and vulgar statement about Ivanka and her microphone at her meeting in Germany. What Waters said was that he liked the way Ivanka SPOKE into her microphone. The liberal media decided that this was a comment about a Lewinsky-style sex act. Truthfully, I too admired the confident and assured way that Ivanka spoke into her microphone. Apparently, the liberal media cannot conceive of an educated woman being able to speak confidently into a microphone without sexual connotations. That is how far the leftists are willing to go in their pursuit of the destruction of free speech from sources different from their own.

Remember when Donald Trump was running for office and the ringmaster, Gloria Allred, led another group of women to the microphone to accuse Trump of sexism? After the election, these women retreated into the woodwork, just as the group that came forward against O'Reilly. We have seen the nasty side of liberal Democrats and they will continue to dig up accusers against any conservative speaker. They don't dig up any proof, just accusations that were not made when they supposedly occurred, but years later when goaded by activists like Allred.

Let me re-emphasize the point about Bill O'Reilly's accusers. Notice that with his removal from Fox News that Gloria Allred and the seemingly irate women who attacked him and hurled the accusations are strangely silent?

Chapter Thirty-Two

Fake News and What's Behind It

In her debate with Trump, Hillary Clinton revealed classified information and Democrats hid under their desks. What Hillary did was on live TV and so there was no question.

In May 2017, the liberal Democrats and their fake news media turned up the attacks of Donald Trump. They continued to speculate that there was collusion between the Trump campaign and Russia even with absolutely no evidence and denials from government investigators.

Next, the *Washington Post* and *New York Times* printed stories about Trump having passed along classified information about ISIS to the Russian Ambassador in a White House meeting. American officials in that meeting quickly denied the accusation, but when the *Washington Post* newsroom heard that the unconfirmed story had attracted a large number of Internet hits they broke out in applause. Their damage had been done and it was time to celebrate.

I spent more than half a century ɿ television, including stints as a news ɿ∪ɪ and as a news director. I worked for a short time for a newspaper after leaving the Navy. In all of that time, I can tell you that I never saw the raw hypocrisy or the outright lies that flow from the mainstream media today. They are so hate filled and pompous that they have stopped trying to hide their bias.

It's not confined to NBC, ABC, CBS, CNN or MSNBC. On June 2, 2017, Shepard Smith said this on Fox news: "Vladimir Putin said that even a three-year-old could have hacked computers" during the election. "Did he have a three-year-old do it?"

That's not news, it is this left-wing jackass' attempt to skew the news.

On May 21, 2017, a group of students at Notre Dame's graduation ceremony rudely walked out as the Vice President of the United States was speaking. These students are sent to college to study, to learn, to show tolerance for opposing opinions. Instead, they are indoctrinated by tenured professors who drink deep from the cup of liberalism. I shudder to think what America will be like as these snowflakes grow into adulthood. The mainstream media does nothing to expose this dumbing down of our people.

Chapter Thirty-Three

For those of you who were still wondering, despite my commentary, if such a thing as the fake news media really exists, you now have the answer. CNN has been caught multiple times inventing fake news. Their hatred of President Trump is so profound they simply cannot miss an opportunity to mislead gullible viewers who still watch them.

Consider the news coverage of the meeting between President Trump and Russian President Vladimir Putin in Germany on July 7, 2017. First, the biased media speculated that the issue of Russian meddling in the 2016 election would not be brought up at all in that meeting. That wasn't news, it was media speculation and it turned out to be wrong.

President Trump did raise the issue when the meeting began and Putin denied any Russian involvement in our election. Putin also asked for any proof Trump had to show Russian involvement.

While the United States, at the Democrats' insistence is spending millions of dollars on multiple investigations looking for that proof, there was no proof to give to Putin.

At that point what was Trump to do? Keep hammering on a subject that Putin had already denied, or try to move past it and seek common ground on the many problems facing our two countries? What purpose would it have served for Trump to argue with Putin about it until the Russian president simply left the room and all discussions?

That is apparently what Senate minority leader Chuck Schumer expected the president to do. Schumer was quick to pop up on the fake news media with condemnation of Trump for discussing anything else with Putin except for the issue of Russian interference in our election.

What about Syria? Isis? Iran? Schumer's indignation was misplaced and highly partisan. He showed again that the leftists in the Democrat party cannot get over Hillary Clinton's loss and that they are so consumed with hate that they are shortsighted and foolish.

Think back to the meeting in Florida between President Trump and the president of China. Schumer and his Democrat posse jumped on Trump for not climbing all over the Chinese president about currency manipulation in that meeting. It was not the time nor the place for such a discussion. President trump was seeking the help of China to rein in the maniac in North Korea, who threatens to touch off World War III.

How then would it have been helpful for Trump to berate the Chinese leader about a subject that was not as pressing as cooperation in the quest to disarm a nuclear North Korea?

The entire democrat response to both meetings was childish and ignorant. Trump may or may not get Chinese help in curbing this maniacal dictator in North Korea but it is certainly worth trying and dealing with currency manipulation at a later time.

The same is true about the meeting between Trump and Putin. How silly is it for the Democrat party and the liberal media to try and dictate the meeting agenda of a lawfully-elected president of the United States. They have no inside knowledge about which subject should dominate the meeting agenda.

In his campaign, Trump made several promises to the American people, but he did not specify, nor should he specify, which of those promises he would deal with first or in what order overall. The political landscape changes daily and a president has to be flexible in confronting those changes.

Politics has always been a nasty business, but over the past two decades it has moved beyond nasty into a world of personal venom. All of that culminated in the election of Donald Trump as president. Liberal Democrat America was smugly counting the days until Hillary Clinton was sure to move into the White House.

So sure were the Democrats that Hillary's victory was in the bag that they never said a word as Hillary took Pennsylvania, Wisconsin. Ohio and Michigan for granted. How could they have gotten it all so wrong? Simple, they underestimated the American people.

The mainstream media has become so careless with their news bias that they lost credibility with the audience. They may never regain it because they show no signs of fairness post-election, and, in fact, they have become more biased and predictable.

Democrats began to float around all kinds of conspiracy claims with absolutely no evidence to back them up. The main claim was that Donald Trump colluded with Russia's Vladimir Putin to swing the election. When government officials announced that they had found no evidence of collusion between Putin and Trump, the liberal Democrats quickly shifted to the conspiracy that "someone" in the Trump campaign had colluded with Russia. They had no name to report nor evidence to back up their fake news claim, but they plowed ahead anyway.

By now, the liberal Democrats were in complete disarray, pointing the blame for Clinton's loss upon one another. But Clinton's defeat was a self-inflicted wound. Democrats had backed a lame horse who could not finish the race. An adult lifetime spent lying and conniving showed her to be less trustworthy than the Grinch who stole Christmas.

And so, Donald Trump would be president. The liberal Democratic community was first stunned, and then vowed to destroy Trump personally and his presidency. As I write this the Trump presidency has existed for 200 days, and during that time there has been a continuous undermining of President Trump's agenda. That's the very agenda that he promised voters who then elected him.

To the liberal critics and media who harped on the fact that Trump had not been able to do all he promised in his first 200 days, I remind them that their obstructionism has delayed the time table. They are like the bully in the playground's sack race who keeps throwing large rocks into the opponent's sack and criticizing him (her) for not being as fast as they said they would be.

Chapter Thirty-Four

After Donald Trump was elected president and he appointed Jeff Sessions as attorney general, Sessions asked for the resignation of 46 politically-appointed attorneys in the federal system. Democrats and the fake news media pretended that this was unusual, when, in fact, it is the norm after an election. All presidents do it to get their own people in place.

Before leaving office, Barack Hussein Obama laid several land mines in the path of the incoming President, all while grinning into the cameras and pretending to make nice. Just before leaving office he used an executive order to open up confidential information to a wide range of government agencies. These agencies, in most cases are still manned by Obama loyalists and we now have seen the leaks of information have become a common occurrence. The reason is that Obama's followers are there to undermine the Trump presidency. The sooner Trump fires these devilish traitors, the sooner the leaks will end.

Don't you get a chuckle from the left wingers like Bernie Sanders, among others, who tell us that the Republican are rushing too quickly to repeal and replace Obamacare when the Democrats themselves rushed far quicker to sign on to Obamacare, before they even read what was in it? At least the Republican proposals are there for all to see.

The demonstrations by women are organized and paid for by billionaire George Soros. Who among us disputes the value of women? This is a bogus argument by radical feminists who Soros is happy to fund. Equal pay for equal work is one of the recurrent themes, but how do we measure equal work? If a man or woman is on a production line it is easy to see what each produces. However, in many jobs it is not that easy. The job title may be the same, but how one performs under the job title can be far different. If a man produces more he should be paid more, and if a woman produces more she should be paid more. Job titles do not dictate the quality of work.

Chapter Thirty-Five

When we see the protestors in the streets, walking out of speeches and repeating the fake news that they hear from the media, it's easy to think that they are simply uninformed. That would be a mistake.

They have been well-informed, indoctrinated if you will, in our schools and universities and by patient socialists and communists who warned us that they would destroy us from within. It's taken decades to bring us to the point of madness, but the time has arrived.

Donald Trump has been doing exactly what the people elected him to do. That agenda, which the voters wanted in place, does not set well with liberal democrats and they reacted in anger and hate. But remember, when they strike out at Trump they are striking out at every American who voted for the man and also against those who chose not to vote because the alternative, Hillary Clinton, left them no choice at all.

Democrats lost all credibility when they tried to derail every single issue that Trump proposed. They lost credibility when they attacked Trump for every bump in the road, as if any president has ever had smooth sailing in the first year of their term.

Certainly, Barack Obama made him mistakes even though he was being pulled by the nose by his Islamic inspired Iranian puppeteer, Valerie Jarrett and allowed himself to be guided by far-left liberals rather than lead himself.

Donald Trump is not without faults, none of us are. He has a broad agenda endorsed by the American people and he has been showing incredible energy in that pursuit. His job has been much harder than other presidents because of the career Democrats who piled on his back and are clinging to his legs to stop his momentum. Even as they pile on Trump's back, these despicable people go to the media to complain that Trump isn't getting enough done. This began even before the man took the oath of office and gets worse with every passing day.

Democrats needed a reason for the defeat of the unethical Hillary Clinton and they seized upon "possible" Russian collusion with the Trump campaign. They had no evidence to back up their charges, but the mainstream media was only too happy to charge forward with the speculation.

As I write this, there are three separate investigations of that unproven claim from Democrats, including the appointment of a Special Investigator. The cost of all of this is enormous and falls upon the 50% of weary taxpayers who must fund it.

When the investigations are complete the truth will see the light of day. Truth is a rare commodity in Washington. I predict that all of these investigations will prove that Trump did not collude with the Russians. Is it possible that Trump was betrayed by someone in the inner circle? Anything is possible, and if that is proven the guilty party(s) should be named and punished to the fullest extent.

What we do know is that nothing the Russians tried to do made a difference in the defeat of Hillary Clinton. We also know that this is not the first time that Russia has tried to interfere with American politics and it will not be the last. But, it is hypocritical to point the finger at Russia as if they are the only ones interfering in another countries' political system. Barack Obama and his Democrat operatives interfered in Israel's election in an attempt to cause the defeat of Benjamin Netanyahu. Obama spent hundreds of thousands of taxpayer dollars to send operatives into Israel in that effort.

Every country in the world that has the capability of hacking into other government systems does it and the United States is no exception. I called for and welcomed the appointment of a Special Investigator to look into any collusion by the Trump campaign and Russia, if only to call the bluff of Democrats. If the investigation determines that the Democrats were on a witch hunt and there is nothing to their claims, they must be held responsible.

The difference in a career Democrat and a rattlesnake if that the Democrat doesn't rattle its tail before it strikes.

Chapter Thirty-Six

The Truth About Obama

What did you do when Barack Obama said that he intended to bring America down to the level of the rest of the world. Not raise us up, bring us down? What did you do when he told us that if the political winds shifted....in other words, if the lie about Islam being a religion of peace was exposed, he would side with Islam instead of America?

Democrats, in search of power, teamed with naïve college age students, Latinos who enjoyed benefits from working Americans, illegal immigrants who were not entitled to vote, but did so in large numbers, and black Americans who let the color of Obama's skin override their lack of information about him. They all banded together to put this man, whose entire background had been sealed away by a court at his insistence, and at a cost of millions of dollars into the presidency.

Looking back on it now can you not see that Barack Hussein Obama was the greatest fraud ever perpetrated on America? Will you not now open your eyes and ears to the truth? We knew nothing about Obama. The mainstream media not only refused to dig into his past but actively sought to discourage those who tried to expose him by calling them "extremists" and worse. It cost a reported $1.7 million dollars to get all of Obama's records sealed from the public. Who put up that money and why? It was far more important for voters to know about Obama's past than to see Trump's personal tax returns.

Obama is out of office, thank God, so we need not waste our time on him now. But the damage he has done, aided and abetted by Harry Reid and Nancy Pelosi, will live on with us. This goes beyond whether or not Obama is a Muslim. His mother and relatives tell us that he is a Muslim. Obama's Father was a Muslim and a child born of a Muslim Father is a Muslim at birth. His Mother registered him for an Islamic school in Indonesia as a Muslim. He got assistance for college expenses in America by claiming to be a foreign student from Indonesia and a Muslim.

Obama's greatest influences in life were Muslims like Frank Davis, himself a communist, and Obama was a devotee of the avowed communist Saul Alinsky, as was Hillary Clinton. His closest White House advisor was Valerie Jarrett, an Iranian and devoted Muslim.

This American president bowed to the King of Saudi Arabia and, under Valerie Jarrett's influence Obama bailed out the Iranian economy by giving the billions of dollars in untraceable cash. He also released five Iranians jailed in the

United States, all for Iran's signature on a bogus agreement to end nuclear construction in that country. The Iranians got the money and never intended to honor the agreement. Those untraceable American dollars gave Iran the ability to continue supporting terrorism around the world. That blood is on the hands of Barack Obama and Valerie Jarrett.

Muslim or not, Obama walks like a duck, quacks like a duck, and hides his true identity from the American people. The grand plan of Obama and liberal Democrats was destroyed when Hillary Clinton was defeated by Donald Trump. The fake news media had been very supportive of Trump when he was in the Republican primary. Those fake news presenters and career Democrats thought that Trump would be easier to defeat, even by their terribly flawed candidate. We had been set up for the kill by the liberal establishment and they needed just one more coronation to complete their scheme.

With Hillary Clinton as president, all of Obama's fundamental changes would be protected and expanded upon. The Supreme Court would be filled with far-left justices like Ruth Bader Ginsberg and the corruption in government would continue unabated.

The liberal Democrats were so full of themselves and their ability to con the American people that they allowed Hillary Clinton, a woman who lies more than an errant golf ball, to be their nominee. This unethical woman has the morality of Judas and is harder to like than a poisonous snake with a pass key to your house. Still, the Democrats let her lead the way and she took them over the cliff. In all honestly, what options did the Democrats have? Just a loony Bernie Sanders or the Pocahontas of the tribe, Elizabeth Warren? That's like choosing between Bin Laden and Jeffrey Dahmer. One will kill you and the other will eat you.

President Donald J. Trump

Chapter Thirty-Seven

Trump's Personal Tax Returns

Even before Donald Trump's first day in office he was harassed by left-leaning groups like MoveOn.Org, Media Matters and other Soros-backed snake pits. These protest marches are well organized events with a core of paid anarchists who attract liberals who are "useful idiots." That's not my phrase, by the way. The Russians coined it to describe wild-eyed liberals, especially of college age, who never question the cause. As Democrat Rahm Emmanuel said years ago, "Never let a crisis go to waste."

The mainstream media focuses on the useful idiots in the march rather than the paid protestors in order to convince us these events are spontaneous. While it is true that not all of the protestors are paid, it is true that those who organize and lead these so-called protests are paid, and well paid. Moreover, they move from protest to protest rather than hold down a real-world job.

Some of these "protests" are comical, such as the marches demanding to see Trump's personal tax returns. Many, if not most of the marchers, pay little or no taxes at all. Many are receiving government assistance of some kind, including unemployment benefits. They have absolutely no evidence about Trump's tax returns, but are eager to find something that those above them can pick at and mischaracterize to keep the anti-Trump campaign in the headlines.

The Internal Revenue system is set up to review all of our tax returns, including those of Donald Trump. If there is something illegal in Trump's returns it is the duty of the IRS to make that known. But no one in the IRS has even suggested that there is anything illegal in Trump's returns. It's not like the IRS has not violated the law themselves in targeting Conservatives or that the head of the IRS is a Democratic flunky who we can trust as much as a faulty bungee cord.

Think of what we face in our world today: Relations with Russia are at an all-time low; we have a maniacal dictator in North Korea testing missiles that could deliver nuclear warheads into America and start a disastrous World War III. Iran supports terrorists and begins each day chanting "DEATH TO AMERICA" and George Soros-backed anarchists are on our streets undermining our president.

Is it more important to see an end to the deadly threats against our people by world dictators and Islamic terrorists or for Donald Trump's personal tax returns to be made public? Trump's tax returns are extremely complicated and lengthy and none of us would understand the returns. What liberal Democrats and the fake news media want is to plow through Trump's returns and, hopefully, find something they can blow out of context to undermine his presidency.

They've done that with all these claims about Russia and the Trump campaign. They have to continue to try and find things that they can keep in the headlines and it does not matter whether there is evidence to support them or not. NBC aired a tape of Donald Trump and Billy Bush a couple of days before Trump's debate with Hillary Clinton. It was designed to put the final nail in Trump's coffin. What many Americans don't know is that NBC had that tape for several years and many executives at the network knew what was in it.

Donald Trump is a prominent businessman whose name is better known than most. Why was the NBC tape not news at the time? Why wait until Trump was near election to the presidency? It was because, as long as Trump was not a danger to the liberal agenda, they'd hide the tape from the public. Is that dishonest? Of course it is, but the simple truth is that the mainstream media long ago lost the people's trust as an unbiased source of news.

Let me say that the private conversation on an NBC bus between Trump and Billy Bush some 12 years ago was crude locker room talk and best left unsaid. Donald Trump is human and human beings make mistakes.

Until Donald Trump can be shown, with evidence, to not be working in our country's best interest we must tell liberal America, the socialists and communists among them, and the useful idiots who tag along, to take a long walk off a short pier and tread water for generations.

Chapter Thirty-Eight

Whether you are a Democrat or a Republican, you should be concerned with what is happening in our country today. I want those of you who have been lifelong Democrats to understand that when I am pointing out the hypocrisy of career Democrats in Washington, I am not speaking of all Democrats.

Never in our history was there such an outpouring of hate directed at a president in his first few months than that directed at Donald Trump. In fact, liberal Democrats began the hate campaign against Trump even before he took office. Anyone who thinks that George Soros, Barack Obama, Hillary Clinton and a few two-faced Republicans are not behind this anti Trump hate campaign is kidding themselves.

What has Trump done so far to warrant this constant hate? The man simply has tried to fulfill the promises he made to the American people while running for the presidency. That was the agenda that Trump was elected on. It's not Trump the man that liberals hate as much as that agenda he was elected to fulfill. Many, if not most, of these hypocritical Democrats, were kissing Trump's ring and begging him for money before he decided to run for office.

Remember, these are the same left wing hypocrites who were attacking Trump because he would not say, prior to the election, that he would or would not support a peaceful transfer of power. Yet, when their designated heir, Hillary Clinton, lost the election they immediately set out to block a peaceful transition of power. How can a rational person support such obvious hypocrites?

Liberal Democrats want open borders and a free flow of immigrants, regardless of our ability to vet them. Donald Trump promised to quash that insanity. He wanted to seal our borders and stop the influx of refugees until such time as we can fully vet them and their intentions in our country.

These are not the immigrants of our forefathers. Those immigrants came here legally. They were vetted at places like Ellis Island in New York, screened for diseases and evaluated as to any burden they would place upon our society. They were not given a free ride when they arrived here, but were expected to fend for themselves and they were thankful for the opportunity.

The immigrants flooding into America today illegally are not the best and brightest. They are not doctors or engineers. They are people, for the most part, who were living day-to-day in their own countries. Of course, they want to come here, but even those who are not extremists become a burden on our economy. No other country in the world offers cash and benefits to refugees as is done in the United States. Other countries, especially Mexico, carefully vet immigrants to make sure that they are admitting people who can care for themselves without calling upon their governments for their livelihood.

President Trump made other promises before his election that touched the hearts and minds of the electorate. Liberal Democrats were convinced that he could never be elected, so they held their hate in check for the moment. Once they saw that America was onto their deceit and the dishonesty of Hillary Clinton, these liberals went ballistic.

They had two options. The first option was to accept a peaceful transfer of power, as they had demanded before the election and put America's interest before that of their political party and to seek ways to find common ground with the new President, rather than oppose every single thing that the President wanted to do. The second option was to launch a campaign of hate. They chose hate.

How can anyone take a politician, Democrat or Republican, who seriously says that they will refuse to meet with the president and will not support ANYTHING he proposes, even before they know what those proposals are? Those vile threats came from the rather loud mouth of

California Democrat Congresswoman, Maxine Waters. Dissent is healthy. Hate is destructive. Maxine Waters has a college degree and yet she exhibits ignorance on a daily basis. She is the poster woman for what our educational system can put out. She can't help her appearance, nature has not been kind, but she can at least shut the mouth that roared.

Chapter Thirty-Nine

What Are They Saying About President Trump?

There is no evidence at all that Donald Trump is a racist and liberal Democrats know it. He got more of the black vote than Democrats expected precisely because he promised to do something about the destruction of the black families and communities, ending drug deals openly on the streets of urban cities and prosecute gang members who terrorize honest, hard-working black Americans in their own neighborhoods.

Trump promised to pursue jobs for the jobless and help black America recover from the dependence on government that Democrats created in order to keep black Americans under control and safely on the political plantations they constructed.

They attacked Trump for being against the Jews, but Trump brought his Jewish son-in-law into a major advisory position in his administration. His daughter, Ivanka, accepted Judaism with her marriage and her Jewish children are Trump's beloved grandchildren.

Trump's background is not sealed away as is Obama's and there is nothing to suggest that he is an anti-Semite. Still, his liberal enemies allied against his policies claiming that he had not been forceful enough in denouncing anti-Semitism.

Does anyone remember Barack Obama or Hillary Clinton denouncing Al Sharpton? Jesse Jackson? Louis Farrakhan? Or the Black Lives Matter crowd that sees nothing wrong with rioting, looting and burning at the slightest provocation, real or imagined? Yet, the hypocrites in the Democratic party were not only not forceful enough in condemnation but refused to combat it at all.

None of us know for certain how good or how bad the Trump presidency will be, but those patriots who love this country more than partisan politics are willing to give the man time to show what he can do.

As for me, I voted for the man because of his promises to bring America back from the brink of ruin that had escalated over the past eight years, and because the Democrats were willing to bet the farm on one of the most deceitful, unethical liars of all time. Had they developed a conscience and presented a different candidate, they may have had a shot at beating Trump, but who could they replace Hillary with? Pelosi? Shumer? Anthony Weiner? Bill DeBlasio? Socialist Bernie or the ghost from Christmas past, Elizabeth Warren?

At the time of this writing, I support every agenda item that President Trump has set forth.

I firmly believe that we will look back on the Trump administration as the turning point of our descent into oblivion. How arrogant it is for liberals to demand that a fair and honest election result be overturned because the result of that election did not please them?

In the fantasy world of liberalism, it is firmly believed that the average, ordinary American is too ignorant to know what's best for them and so it is up to liberals among us to save us from our ignorance. Whether or not you voted for Donald Trump, it should deeply concern you when any group of people unite to circumvent the votes of the American people.

I have no love for either of our main political parties because each side is stacked with career politicians to whom greed and power is far more important that the stability of our country. I do generally vote for Republicans because I am a Conservative who has seen the dangers of the left.

It bothers me that the Republican party also has obstructionists like Lindsay Graham of South Carolina and John McCain of Arizona. Both secretly want Trump to fail and it is these two who the media trots out to say that "some Republicans agree with the Democrats." By wishing for Trump to lose they would foist Hillary Clinton into the Presidency. With friends like that Trump needs no enemies.

Democratic House minority leader, Nancy Pelosi from the far, far left area of San Francisco recently said in May 2017 that, so far, she had not seen anything that President Bush has proposed that she can support. President Bush?

In late May, she criticized President Trump's visit to the Middle East because he went to Saudi Arabia instead of visiting the countries alphabetically. The same gig dong who told us that they had to sign Obamacare quickly so they could know what was in it. Yogi Berra is spinning in his grave.

We must recognize that life is not a game to be played out between political hacks. The world is more dangerous today than at any time in human history. I'll take good old common sense over all of those pompous, over-educated individuals who look down their noses at the average, ordinary Americans that are the backbone of our great country. Remember when Hillary's campaign manager, John Podesta, posted an email saying that Hillary hated average, ordinary Americans?

We must reject the liberal Democrat onslaught against this president. Give him a chance to follow up on his promises to us. It is those promises that he was elected to fulfill and it is those same promises that liberal Democrats fear will reverse the course of America from the disaster of Barack Obama. If Trump is a successful president, America wins; but the career politicians of the far-left lose and that is something they must destroy.

I honestly believe it was the hand of God that tipped the scales in the 2016 election of Donald Trump. (I'll pause a moment here for liberal Democrats to clutch their chest and take a valium.) We were given one last chance to save ourselves and our country. The election was in the bag for Clinton. Media pundits were gleeful while telling us there was only a slim chance that Trump could prevail and that chance was slimmer than Rosie O'Donnell disarming her body guards. It would take an act of God for Hillary to lose and that is exactly what happened.

Chapter Forty

I remember very well what I was thinking about as the transition from Barack Obama to Donald Trump in the Oval Office was about to take place. Just four days before President Trump's inauguration, I broadcast a commentary on the subject. Here is what I said:

In just four days Barack Hussein Obama will leave the White House as an ex-President. He will not go away from the national stage because this self-inflated man has far too much ego for that exit. While George Bush refused to question Obama for eight years, Obama has sent signals that he intends to second guess Donald Trump and keep his nose in the country's business.

It has always been a mystery to me how Obama promised to fundamentally change America by bringing it down to the level of the rest of the world rather than raise it up. Yet, he ended up with enough delusional followers who refused to see the damage he brought upon us.

Even as he was winding down his disastrous presidency, Barack Obama appeared before our troops at McDill Air Force base to praise Islam and to urge the troops to question Donald Trump as president. Many of our top Generals were forced out of the military for questioning Obama and yet this hypocrite suggests that our military men and women should question a president?

Obama came into office with a trail of lies. He blatantly used the color of his skin to con black Americas into supporting him as the first black president. He used the color of his skin to keep criticism of his policies muted. He promised to heal the great divide between the races and yet, in office, he did nothing to better the lives of blacks and, instead of healing the divide, he widened it further.

Now, he says that the color of his skin is what people in the south focused on. Frankly, we noticed the color of his skin only when he was using it as a cover. Barack Obama was born a Muslim. Anyone who follows Islam remains a Muslim for life. Leaving Islam is punishable by death. Obama was enrolled in school by his mother as a Muslim. He was mentored by communists and Muslims. He got into college using a foreign student status to gain aid and roomed with two radical Muslims. His church of choice was pastored by Jeremiah Wright, a man with a determined hate for America.

Obama sat through some 20 years of sermons from Wright, sermons that ranged from mild rebuke for this country to wild screaming and the cursing of America. Obama says that in 20 years of attendance he never heard any of this from Wright. Talk about sleeping in church.

As President Obama chose a Muslim, Valerie Jarrett, with deep ties to Iran, as his top advisor and then proceeded to bring members of the Muslim Brotherhood into his administration, some in sensitive national security areas.

Upon his election as president, Obama set out on a world tour where he apologized for America and all it stood for. He bowed to the Muslim King of Saudi Arabia and told us that our country owed a debt to Islam for what Islam had contributed to the world and to our society, but left out the part about Muslim atrocities and their stated aim to dominate the world. Exactly what have Muslims contributed to the world in the last 500 years? Obama did not specify. He instead refused to even acknowledge that Islamic terrorism even exists.

It really doesn't matter whether or not Obama admits to being a Muslim. What does matter is how he defended Muslim positions, that he surrounded himself with Muslim advisors, and bowed to Muslim leaders. It matters that Obama was responsible for allowing Muslim refugees into this country who are not fully vetted and that he supports sanctuary cities that provide a safe hiding place for the criminals and terrorists among them.

It matters that Obama chose not to address the issue of illegal immigrants who have been deported from this country and who return to bring in drugs, commit rapes and murders. Two American women were recently killed by an illegal immigrant who had been deported 8 times, EIGHT times.

Rahm Emmanuel, an Obama insider and Mayor of Chicago has promised to keep that city a sanctuary haven for illegal immigrants. He said that he would offer safety to them in his city and yet the man can't even provide safety for his own citizens. Weekly shootings and killings in Chicago continue to escalate. Rahm Emmanuel is a cruel joke and Chicago is a cesspool of depravity.

There are no words to describe fully the damage that Obama's eight years of dictatorial policies did to our country; beginning with the monstrous rate increases to occur this year for Obamacare and the fact that the whole Obamacare mess will implode in 2017. We will be decades digging out of the hole that Obama dug for us.

Obamacare was structured to collapse after Obama left office. He, Hillary Clinton and liberal Democrats wanted a government-run national health system and with the death of Obamacare they thought that Hillary Clinton, as president, could push that through. We need only look at the debacle of healthcare offered to our veterans in VA hospitals to see the danger of a government-run healthcare system for all Americans.

Average, ordinary Americans rose up to keep Clinton out of the White House and to destroy the deceitful legacy of Barack Hussein Obama. A businessman, Donald Trump, was elected president. Liberal Democrats were stunned. The mainstream media, who had done all possible to get Hillary elected, hyperventilated and turned then to negativity about a Trump presidency that had not even begun. So-called "stars" of Hollywood reneged on their promises to leave the country if Trump was elected. They chose instead to second guess the American people who elected Trump and to demean the man the people had elected. On the abominable show, *The View* on ABC, the far-left liberal Joy Behar said that Trump was out of his head.

Denzel Washington said it best when he said that if we choose not to watch, listen, or read the news we are uninformed and if we do watch, listen, or read the news we are misinformed.

The most important thing that keeps me researching and commentating on the news after these 54 years is my desire to bring you the truth. To inform and not misinform. I can tell you that it is frustrating on the one hand to hear from people who are in complete denial of the facts on a given subject, unwilling to re-examine their loyalties to political parties, and stuck in the past.

On the other hand, it is gratifying to hear from those who want to see light rather than remain stuck in the darkness. Those who seek the truth, even when it upsets something they had long believed, and those who are willing to give a president, even a president they did not vote for, the time in office to show whether the vote was right or wrong. I cannot belong to either of our two major political parties.

I began as a Democrat because my family were Democrats and before that party's far-left elites hijacked it and top loaded it with leftists like Nancy Pelosi, Chuck Schumer, Bernie Sanders and Elizabeth Warren. I then became a Republican, but the failure of Republicans to follow through on promises made to correct the course of our country, even when in the majority, caused me to register as an Independent around 2000. I am a Conservative, so I vote Republican most of the time. However, in the past, I have contributed money and voted for some Democrats, but as long as the Democrat party stands behind the far left I can't support them.

That brings me back to the frustration I feel when people who are registered Democrats refuse to acknowledge that the party is no longer the same party they expected when they registered to vote. Their family members, who were long time Democrats, would not be in line today with the extreme far-left movement that is destroying the Democrat party. They themselves don't share the vision of Democrat elites like Sanders and Warren, but it is much easier to stay in denial than to confront the truth.

Chapter Forty-One

World history is replete with stories of great civilizations who fell from grace and toppled into despair. Perhaps the Roman Empire is the greatest of those who lost it all. They took on far too much debt, listened to the voices of the strident left, overextended their military and are but a memory.

Our military today is the weakest since the beginning of World War II. Our Navy is no longer the greatest naval power. We are ripe for the taking except for the millions of Americans who possess firearms and who have the patriotism to use them against any assault upon America. Obama has said that his greatest regret is that he was not able to impact our right to keep and bear arms. Hillary Clinton, too, is on record with her desire to ban guns for American citizens. She denies that in public, but supports it in private.

During World War II, a Japanese military officer said that the only reason they did not invade the American homeland was because there was a rifle behind every blade of grass. Liberals would take away those rifles and mow down the grass to where our enemies could better see us.

I will repeat again that I have no way of knowing how good or bad Donald Trump will be as our president and neither does anyone else, including those in fantasy land who know as little as we do but pretend to know it all. What we do know is that when a nation practices evil there is no way it will be blessed in the long run.

We have become a nation that is dripping with corruption and wickedness from the top to the bottom. In the end, you always reap what you sow. The days of reckoning are here and if we are unable to reverse Obama's fundamental changes designed to bring our country down, the future will not be pretty.

We have long needed a president, be they black or white, man or woman, who understands the basics of business. For decades, our leaders in Washington have pushed us towards a global economy and told us it would be good for us. But, there is a flip side. Now workers in the United States must compete with workers all over the world and our greedy corporations are free to pursue the cheapest labor available anywhere on the globe.

Millions of jobs have already been shipped out of the United States and Princeton University economist Alan Blinder estimates that 22-29% of all current jobs will be offshore within the next decade unless changes are made. The days when blue collar workers could live the American dream are gone and they will not come back unless we reject the status quo offered by people like Barack Obama, Hillary Clinton, or even entrenched old-timers in the Republican party who lead the House and Senate.

Beyond terrorism our greatest problem is debt. Collectively, the U.S. government, state governments, corporate America and American consumers have accumulated the greatest mountain of debt in the history of the world. Still, Obama was able to get Congress to raise the debt ceiling again and again until we are now $20 TRILLION in national debt. Democrats supported allowing Obama to increase the debt, but Republicans also bear a share of the blame for not doing more to block it.

Meanwhile, the horrendous waste of taxpayer money by the federal government has been documented, but has not been stopped by Congress. Large monetary grants are given out for ridiculous reasons, such as studies to watch how shrimp react on a treadmill or money to see the effects of cigarettes on mice. We all heard about the hammers and toilet seats that the Pentagon was buying at hundreds of dollars each. It doesn't take an accountant to see that someone, or many someones, are getting kickbacks and fleecing the taxpayers.

When these things are brought to light there is a short outburst of concern, but no follow up in the mainstream media. That allows the thieves to stop buying the hammers and toilet seats and move on to the next rip-off.

The reality is that we are being sucked into an economic black hole from which our economy may never fully recover. The U.S. government is now in charge of the largest Ponzi scheme in history. We are facing a pension crisis of unprecedented magnitude. Virtually all pension funds in the United States, both public and private, are massively underfunded. With millions of baby boomers getting ready to retire, there is simply no way on earth that all of these obligations can be met.

Robert Marx of the University of Chicago and Joshua Rauh of Northwestern's Kellogg School of Management calculated that the collective unfunded pension liability for all 50 U.S. states at more than $40 trillion dollars. Social Security and Medicare, and Medicaid expenses, are wildly out of control. Perfectly healthy Americans are filing disability claims in record numbers. Just thinking of all of this is depressing, but not understanding the problem is even worse.

The reckless expansion of the money supply by the U.S. government and the Federal Reserve is going to end up destroying the U.S. dollar and the value of the remaining net worth of all Americans if change does not come soon. The more dollars there are available, the less each individual dollar is worth. In essence, inflation is like a hidden tax on each dollar that you owe. When they flood the economy with money, the value of the money in your bank account goes down.

U.S. economic growth depends upon shoppers and those shoppers are not spending at the same rate as years before. American factories are suffering from a global economic slowdown. Manufacturing makes up ten percent of the U.S. economy, according to Morgan Stanley. The key ISM manufacturing index has declined for six straight months and it's been negative, below 50%, for the last two months.

The strong dollar is making products manufactured in the U.S. more expensive overseas, lowering demand for American-made goods. The slowdown in emerging market economies isn't helping trade either. American companies are making less money than a year ago. Put together, when America's biggest companies and employers suffer, the economy follows suit. Poor people don't hire others, corporations do.

I say all of this to point out the need for a president who understands business; a president who has at their beck-and-call the financial and business experts who can help guide a turnaround. What we have had for many years has been presidents content with the status quo in Washington.

Whether or not you supported or voted for Trump, you cannot deny that the man knows the business world. His successes in business have been such that liberal Democrats are demanding

Tom Joyner

that he divest his business interests to avoid any conflict of interest. Most, if not all, in Congress have conflicts of interest every day. Remember, it was not that long ago that public outrage stopped members of Congress from attaining wealth through insider trading, something the rest of us would be sent to prison for doing. Most members of Congress want to be on select committees. In those closed-door committee hearings, they are many times privy to inside information about some business merger, a new product development, or a huge company sale. A quick call to their stock broker with that inside information could make a Congressperson a millionaire overnight. It went on for decades before someone finally blew the whistle on it and the resulting publicity caused Congress to take measure to prevent insider trading from Capitol Hill.

Nancy Pelosi's husband has benefitted greatly in his business due to Pelosi's position in Congress. This is true of both Democrats and Republicans. Democrats seem to forget that John F. Kennedy was very wealthy. His father, "Ole Joe" Kennedy had made millions bootlegging during the depression and yet JFK was never asked to divest any business interest or to show how his father would not benefit financially from JFK's role as President. JFK named his brother Robert to the attorney general position and yet no Democrat asked Robert Kennedy to divest any business interest or to show why his role as

168

attorney general would not financially benefit the Kennedy family financially. John F. Kennedy and Robert Kennedy's brother, Ted, was in a key position in the Senate at the same time and yet no Democrat or mainstream media sources questioned how it could be that the Kennedys, holding three key positions in government, including the most powerful office in the world, would not benefit from JFK's presidency.

It was well known in Washington and in Austin, Texas that Democrat Lyndon Johnson was not honoring his agreement to place his financial interests in a blind trust. Johnson went so far as to personally call advertisers in Austin from the White House on behalf of Johnson's radio and televisions stations there. He held off other broadcast competition by strong-arming the Federal Communication Commission (FCC) and it was only after LBJ left the White House that more than eight competitive radio stations were allowed into the Texas capitol, more than double the number of competitors against the Johnson family stations.

Then we come to Bill and Hillary Clinton. No Democrat questioned the charges of pay-to-play against Hillary Clinton regarding the Clinton Foundation. Millions of dollars poured into the foundation while Hillary was secretary of state. These were called "donations" and it was only after Hillary Clinton lost the presidency to Donald Trump that those "donations" dried up. When she lost power, nobody was inviting Bill

Clinton to speak to them for $500,000 dollars anymore.

It is extreme hypocrisy for Democrats to claim that Trump's businesses might benefit from his presidency. If Trump moves this country forward, we all benefit.

The greatest benefit of the Trump presidency can provide us is appointees to the Supreme Court. With the death of Justice Antonin Scalia liberals were celebrating the opportunity for Hillary Clinton to appoint another far-left justice like Ruth Bader Ginsberg to the court and let the court legislate from the bench rather than follow the U.S. Constitution. This would have skewed the Supreme Court to the far-left for decades. We dodged that bullet with the election of Donald Trump. He gave us a list of judges he would consider for the court. Hillary Clinton declined to produce such a list. Democrats can try to excuse Clinton's loss to Trump by talking about Russian hacking and I don't, for a minute, think that the Russians did not hack into John Podesta's email; but that's not why Clinton lost the White House. Did the Russians cause her to lose to Obama as well?

As I wrote the above for a commentary, it was four days before we had our new president in the White House. True patriots will unite behind him and give him time to prove his ability to move this country forward. Those filled with hate will protest, parade, loot and burn. They are not patriots, they are anarchists. Conservatives, of which I am one, tolerated Barack Obama without resorting to violence on a grand scale. The intolerant liberals called for boycotts and protests even before our 45th President took office and they vow to continue their disruptive practices for the length of Trump's term in office.

They know that there will be violence while marching under the liberal umbrella, but their naked greed for power is more important to them than their country.

Donald Trump certainly has his character flaws, just as you and I do. He shoots from the hip sometimes with his words, but it is his actions in office, not words, that will determine whether or not Trump is a successful president.

He will be opposed at every step by a greedy and deceitful national Democrat party, and he will be undercut by RINO's like John McCain and Lindsay Graham who are bitter because the candidate they preferred did not win.

Trump will be the most transparent president in our history. He says what is on his mind and that is why Trump is right to keep his Twitter account active; to use it to reach out to the American people who want the truth, not the left-wing biased fake news offered by the mainstream media. To be sure, Trump needs to confine his Twitter remarks to the tasks at hand and learn to let his critics take their cheap shots at him without personally firing back. Let his surrogates do that for him. He has to choose his battles and let the petty stuff pass him by.

We are in a new age of communication whereby a president can reach out to tens of millions of Americans and go over the heads of fake news media organizations who work diligently to undermine conservatism. Just as the Pony Express gave way to telephone lines and fax machines, so does Trump's Twitter account move him beyond a dependence upon a dishonest, biased mainstream media.

The extreme left in America has seen the roller coaster they had us on stopped in its tracks and that has them reacting with hate like a caged bear being poked with a sharp stick. They are not open to a different path from liberalism. They had God, morality, and truth on the ropes, and with Hillary Clinton's loss they face a reversal of their agenda. If Trump stays the course, fulfills his promises, and puts America first, his critics will soon be overrun by believers. There is hope and there will be change; just not the changes liberals had hoped for.

Chapter Forty-Two

Since I have referred to President Trump's business background, I thought it is appropriate to discuss a significant evolution in technology that could change America's job landscape as we know it.

I almost left this information out of the book because it is deep technology and the average, ordinary American, myself included, can get a headache just muddling through the verbiage, not to mention the fear of the possibilities. However, it is something we need to be aware of and follow. I'm referring to the evolving phenomenon known as "artificial intelligence."

Who knew that a machine would handle the order for a burger at McDonald's? The Japanese now have shopping carts that scan your grocery buys and check you out quickly. The possibilities are endless.

Most Americans have no thoughts on the matter of artificial intelligence because it has not been on the media's radar screen. They spend their time undermining President Trump rather than providing us with the information we need to understand the pros and cons of artificial intelligence. I find it ironic that we are discussing artificial intelligence when there is so little human intelligence left in the world.

What I am about to say will be easier to understand if you substitute the term "robots" for artificial intelligence. In my research on the subject, I came across information from several experts on the subject, but the most informative was Rick Blaisdell and I give him credit.

Many times in history, the human imagination has given birth to former science-fiction fantasies. From pocket computers to self-driving cars, space tourism, virtual reality, and now, artificial intelligence, humanity has blurred the lines of fantasy and fiction through innovation and curiosity.

Artificial Intelligence, abbreviated AI, is now a very real prospect that companies are focusing on. For those of you, like myself, who are still new to this concept, AI is a field of science which focuses on how hardware and software components of a machine can exhibit intelligent behavior. Instead of being fed information by the user himself, they learn over the course of time and become more intelligent. Currently, there are many companies working on AI projects including Microsoft, Google, Facebook and Mindcraft. South Korea also has some high-profile AI in development and these are just the companies that have made their projects public.

Let's not forget that there are probably other companies and countries that are secretly working on Artificial Intelligence projects.

Today, AI, which was once thought to live purely in the human imagination, is very real. In recent months, AI has emerged as a topic of great interest for many leaders of the high tech industry. First, there was Steven Hawking, then Elon Musk and Bill Gates. All of these smart people have suggested that AI is something to watch carefully.

When Tesla CEO, Elon Musk was asked about AI, he said it was like summoning a demon who shouldn't be called unless it can be controlled. When Stephen Hawking was asked the same question he cautioned the public, saying that any further advancement to AI could be a fatal mistake. He mentioned that AI has the power to redesign itself and take off on its own, whereas humans have slow biological evolution and would not be able to compete.

According to Bill Gates, AI devices will be fine initially, but as they start learning more and more from us, and about us, they will get more powerful and intelligent than mankind. There are four classes of risk posed by AI:

First, the only two feasible scenarios by which a maliciously hostile AI might be possible are if it is deliberately programmed to be hostile, perhaps by a military or terrorist group, or if humanity's existence or behavior is actively and deliberately contradicting one of the AI's goals so effectively that the only way to achieve that goal is to wage war on humanity until either humanity's will or capability to resist is destroyed. Next, there is effectively no risk of apathetic danger for AI with a friendliness super goal, but it is almost unavoidable from AI without that goal.

An apathetic AI is dangerous simply because it does not take human safety into account as all humans naturally do. For example, without friendliness goals, an AI in charge of dusting crops with pesticides will dust a field even if it knows that the farmer is still standing in the field inspecting his plants at that moment.

Additionally, an AI, or robot, working with incomplete data is capable of misjudging just like a human. Mistakes of this sort are almost inevitable since it is impossible to know everything there is to know about the world, but they are also the least dangerous of the four risks. Since AI's can learn from their experiences, the occurrence of accidents actually decreases the chance that the mistake will happen again, improving the AI and making it safer.

The real danger of well-designed artificial intelligence is in its ability to reprogram and upgrade itself. Any AI capable of self-improvement is likely to eventually surpass the constraints of human intelligence. Once an AI exists which is smarter than any human it will be literally impossible for any human to fully understand it. Such an AI is also likely to continue improving itself at an exponential rate, making it increasingly impossible to comprehend or predict. Also, at some point, the AI may discover laws of causality or logic far beyond the comprehension of human minds and the possibility of what it can do becomes literally endless. While there are a lot of assumptions about AI being dangerous, we have to remember that these are just assumptions and not clear facts.

Humans have always been doubtful about new technologies and there was a time when we were all hesitant about cell phones. After all, its about how we create AI and how we keep it under control. Researchers have made a wide range of estimates for how far we are from super-human artificial intelligence, but we certainly can't say with great confidence that the probability is zero in this century, given the dismal track record of such predictions.

For example, Ernest Rutherford, arguably the greatest nuclear physicist of his time, said in 1933, less than 24 hours before the invention of the nuclear chain of reaction, that nuclear energy was ridiculous and astronomer Royal Richard Wooley called interplanetary travel utter bilge in 1956.

The most extreme form of this myth is that superhuman AI will never arrive because it's physically impossible. However, physicists know that a brain consists of quarks and electrons arranged to act as a powerful computer and there is no law of physics preventing us from building even more intelligent quark blobs.

There's also a related myth that people who worry about artificial intelligence think it's only a few years away. In fact, most people on record worrying about AI guess that it is still at least decades away, but they argue that as long as we are not 100% sure that it will not happen in this century it's smart to start safety research now to prepare for the eventuality.

Many of the safety problems associated with human-level AI are so hard that they may take decades to solve, so it's prudent to start researching them now rather than the before some programmers drinking Red Bull decide to switch one on.

In the near term, the goal of keeping artificial intelligence impact on society beneficial motivates research in many areas from economics and law to technical topics, such as verification, validity, security, and control. Whereas it may be a little more than a nuisance if your laptop crashes or gets hacked, it becomes all the more important that an AI system does what you want it to do if it controls your car, your airplane, your pacemaker, your automated trading system or your power grid.

Another short-term challenge is preventing a devastating arms race in lethal autonomous weapons. In the long term, an important question is what will happen if the quest for strong artificial intelligence succeeds and an AI system becomes better than humans at all cognitive skills? As pointed out by I.J. Good in

1965, designing smarter AI systems is itself a cognitive task. Such a system could potentially undergo recursive self-improvement, triggering an intelligence explosion leaving human intellect far behind.

By inventing revolutionary new technologies, such as super intelligence, it might help us eradicate war, disease, and poverty, and so the creation of strong AI might be the biggest event in human history. Those cute little robots you can now buy to serve you drinks or vacuum your floors may one day rise up to surpass human intelligence and take over jobs that are already scarce. It's a Catch-22 and we won't know the outcome for decades.

Chapter Forty-Three

The June 2017 shootings in the Alexandria ballpark where Republicans were practicing for a baseball game should have come as no surprise. We have people in our country who are mentally on the edge and the violence being put forth against Republicans and President Trump moves some over the edge.

Such was the case when Bernie Sanders supporter and campaign volunteer, Democrat James Hodgkinson, took his hatred out on innocent Congressmen on a baseball field. This man had a history of violence and had peppered his local Illinois paper with vile comments about President Trump.

Consider that this man was so consumed with Republican hatred that he camped outside of the ballpark in his van to scout the field and plan his slaughter. The field had only one way in and out and this madman began firing on the players and trying to herd them into a position where they were sitting ducks with no escape. It is known that the District of Columbia bans guns and so the Congressmen do not carry arms and would not be armed on that faithful day in June.

They do not have secret service protection and so there would be no protection from that source.

What this liberal shooter did not contemplate is that Louisiana Representative Steve Scalise did have security as a ranking Republican. Two members of the Capitol police moved in on the 66-year-old shooter as he indiscriminately fired away at his hated and defenseless Republicans. Thanks to the bravery of the policeman and police woman confronting him, the shooter was hit and went down. He later died of his wounds at the hospital.

When liberal Democrats call for "blood in the streets," and other violence against Republicans and against President Trump, it is easy to see how a loyal liberal follower could become unhinged and turn to the violence being bandied about. Democrats point to some of the rhetoric from Trump, but Trump has never called for "blood in the streets." At worst, he spoke up for a campaign follower who punched a protester, and while he obviously should not have done that, it remains true that he has not called for killings and "blood in the streets."

Far-left so-called celebrities like Madonna, Kathy Griffin, Rosie O'Donnell, Robert DiNiro and others have called for violent acts against the president. Madonna mused about her thoughts of bombing the White House. Career Democrat politicians are constantly claiming that Republicans want dirty air and water and want to kill children and the elderly. They claim

Republicans want to take health care away and give tax breaks to the rich at the expense of the poor. With that kind of incitement, how does a troubled mind remain sane?

I have researched this rhetoric from Republicans and Democrats. While there have been instances of Republicans demeaning Democrats, the Republican rhetoric does not come close to rivaling the calls for violence from Democrats.

Following the shootings in Alexandria, the liberal Democrats began their predictable chant to keep Americans from having access to guns. While I have no problem with strengthening our gun laws, it would do no good if the laws are not enforced, as is the case with the laws already on the books. My blood pressure rises when I hear politicians and celebrities with armed bodyguards calling for the rest of us to go unarmed. If any of the Republicans on that baseball field had been armed to protect themselves this assault would not have gone on for as long as it did. Those who wish to harm us count on our not being armed. Taking away our guns will not affect their ability to arm themselves.

I first began hunting with my grandfather's 16-gauge shotgun when I was 10 years old. I was taught how to use the gun safely. I've had a concealed carry permit for as long as North Carolina has allowed it. In 65 years, I have never shot at or harmed another human being with a gun. I will never surrender my only real means to protect myself and my family. If that makes me a "gun nut" in the eyes of the liberal community, so be it. Better to face their scorn than to meekly beg an armed criminal for my life.

Chapter Forty-Four

Just pondering the issue of artificial intelligence is so hard to digest, I thought it was appropriate to take a break from such serious topics and visit some more wisdom from Clyde Rambo.

"Me and the misses, that's her over there on the couch, we are thinking about getting a smaller abode ever since the dog died, cause there ain't but the two of us now. I been lookin' on the TV for somebody to help us find a place and I have to wonder about that outfit that flies around in a balloon sellin' houses. First of all, I like to go in a house and check it out before buyin' the thing and how do you do that while flittin' from cloud-to-cloud in a balloon? Maybe I'm missing something here, but it just seems to me it's a whole lot safer to keep your tennis shoes on the ground while pickin' out your property. If you do go the route of the balloon, it might pay you to call Jake at State Farm."

"Given what I see of college students interviewed on the TeeVee, I am glad that I missed the opportunity of goin' into debt to learn nothing. It is pitiful to watch these snowflakes melt before the camera. 'What is the Alamo?' somebody asks and the answer they give is that it's a rental car company. Who did the United States fight in World War II is the question and the answer is France. Course there is a little truth in that one since we had to fight to keep Pierre from cutting tail and runnin' off. These folks go to school for four years and come out thinking that pain reliever is something you get in a divorce. Now they want safe places on campus so they can snivel in private. Save your money. Send Junior to a trade school and git the basement ready."

"Do y'all reckon that George Washington did throw that silver dollar across the Potomic like they say? See, if he did, and we could find that that buck, we could sell it on Ebay for more money than Bill Clinton paid Paula Jones to settle her suit that arose when he couldn't get her to take off her suit. George Washington was a patriot, I don't argue with that, but it would take a mighty heave to get that silver dollar over the river. I have been to Mt. Vernon and looked across that river where he threw the money and maybe in those days a dollar went further than it

185

does now. Just givin' George the benefit of the doubt, don't you see."

"My friend Harvey Pipkin told me he was in the dentist's office yesterday when this couple rushed and said they was on vacation and in a hurry. The woman told the dentist that she wanted a tooth pulled without Novocain, cause they was in a hurry. 'Just yank the tooth out as quick as you can and we'll be out of here,' she told him. Harvey said the dentist told her that she was one courageous woman. 'Which tooth is it?' he asked her. The woman turned around to her husband and said, 'Show him your tooth, dear.'"

"People say the dangdest things. Lucille French went with her husband Willie when he went to his doctor for his annual checkup. The doctor hit Willie on the knee with that little rubber hammer and Willie coughed while the doctor held that cold hearin' thing against his chest. Willie sat quietly while the doctor strapped them little wire thingies on his chest to see if he was goin' to live long enough to get back to his car. Lucille just stood there watchin' and when the doctor finished he called Lucille over and told her that he didn't like the way Willie looked. Lucille said that she didn't either, but he was mighty handy around the house.

"I was in court the other day for a speedin' ticket and there was this lawyer feller cross examining a witness. He said, 'Ain't it true that that you were given five hundred dollars to throw this case? The witness didn't answer, he just stared out the window. So, the attorney repeated the question. Still the witness just stared out the window. Finally, the judge spoke up and and said, 'Please answer the question.' The witness was startled and he said, 'I'm sorry, your honor I thought he was askin' you?'"

On that one, I guess it's time to let Clyde Rambo go back into retirement.

Chapter Forty-Five

More Democrat Hypocrisy

Democrats have tried to impeach Donald Trump practically from the moment he took over the Oval Office. Then, they began chanting "Russia...Russia...Russia," claiming collusion between the Trump campaign and Russia, with absolutely no evidence to base the chant on.

When that failed to gain ground, even with the fake news media treating it like a real news story, they frantically searched for another red herring to float upstream. When Trump defended himself against the daily personal attacks by the hosts of the Morning Joe show on MSNBC with a Tweet, the Democrats and their cohorts in the fake news media went crazy. The hypocrisy exhibited by the left went beyond crazy.

First, they called for impeachment over the Tweet and said that it was beneath a president. How ironic. These are the same people who defended against the impeachment of Bill Clinton when it was revealed that he had engaged in sexual misconduct with a White House intern. Not once, but several times, including trysts with a cigar. Monica Lewinsky was not the first woman to fall under Bill's oversized libido, but she was the only one to have absolute proof when she produced a blue dress with Clinton's DNA on it. Until the dress showed up, Bill was denying his actions and Hillary was calling Lewinsky a loony tune.

Democrats gathered on the Capitol steps to protest against justice being leveled against Clinton and said that what he did was a personal thing and had nothing to do with being president. A personal Tweet by Trump fuels the Democratic hate and, all of the sudden, it is a presidential thing.

Democrats rallied around Ted Kennedy when he drove his car off a Massachusetts bridge, swam to shore and left a young woman in his campaign to drown. Kennedy ran for President. How was that heinous act "presidential?" Yet, not one Democrat made an issue of it.

Anthony Weiner, a Democratic Congressman, solicited minors and send them nude pictures of himself as "Carlos Danger." Democrats stayed mum about Weiner's transgressions because he was married to Hillary's top aide, the Iranian, Huma Abedin. When "Carlos" kept sending his nasty self in pictures to minors and got picked up by authorities, Democrats were strangely silent. Then, when evidence showed that Abedin, Hillary's top aide, had been sending classified documents to Weiner's computer from the

Clinton campaign, Democrats scurried under cover like rat's on a sinking ship.

When Presidential candidate Hillary Clinton called millions of Americans a "basket of deplorables," Democrats flinched but kept quiet. Was that presidential?

When Hillary lied about causing four deaths of Americans in Benghazi and erased 30,000 emails AFTER Congress warned her not to destroy evidence, was that presidential? John Podesta's hacked emails showed that Hillary Clinton hates average, ordinary Americans, but not one Democrat backed off of their support for her. Was that presidential?

When Debbi-Wasserman-Schultz of the Democratic National Committee, and Donna Brazile, passed questions to be asked at the debate between Trump and Clinton, and Clinton accepted them, was that presidential?

Then came the claims that Trump was mentally unfit to be president and had to be impeached. It should be known that Trump has the highest IQ of our presidents and is carrying out the agenda that the American people elected him to do. It is that agenda, not Trump's mental acumen, that these Democratic ne'er-do-wells oppose.

Consider the people in the Democrat party who raise the questions of mental health and who lies: Democrats like Maxine Waters, Nancy Pelosi, Chuck Schumer, Hillary Clinton, Bernie Sanders, Elizabeth Warren, Susan Rice, Elijah

Cummings, Sheile Jackson-Lee, Lois Lerner, "Carlos Danger", and a host to hypocrites like them.

For my part, I hope that President Trump will continue to use Twitter to reach past the fake news media and get his message to the people, but he should not post personal spat issues. That's what the Democrat's want. They bait him and Trump is a street fighter. He survived in a rough and tumble business world that these Democrats could never master. It's his nature to hit back when attacked and I understand that, but he has to learn that in politics you don't always say what you think.

Check Hillary and her "basket of deplorables" debacle. I think that all of us would feel the need to fight back against personal insults, like those hurled at Trump each day on the Morning Joe show from MSNBC, but Trump must understand that this show is rated just below an agricultural propaganda film from North Korea and has fewer viewers than the PA system at a small-town Baptist church. Ignore them. The rest of America does, with the few exceptions of far-left liberals with no conscience.

As for the Republican healthcare draft, it is only a draft and deserves input from ALL members of Congress. Yet, the Democrats offer no solutions, just ignorant rantings. Even these Democrats acknowledge that Obamacare needs changes, but none of them have presented Congress with the changes they claim are needed. They have watched Obamacare unravel for more than seven years and did nothing to make changes that they now say were needed. Hypocritical!

I understand dissent from an opposing political party, but the Democrat party has been hijacked by the extreme left headed by Bernie Sanders and Elizabeth Warren. They offer no agenda of their own, but rely solely on hate, street violence and turmoil. America deserves better. Disagree with Republicans if you like, but they are the only party offering solutions. If you are a Democrat, reread this chapter and ask yourself why these hypocrites speak for you.

Chapter Forty-Six

Mentioning Bernie Sanders brought back memories of the so-called debates between him and Hillary. While they took a few swipes at each other, it was mainly a love-fest for a far-left liberal agenda. Take a look at what a pop-culture, liberal-agenda media has given us.

Recently, I had a chance to look back at old newspaper pictures of Americans around 1900. These folks, black and white, wore their nicest clothes every day. Men wore ties and ladies wore dresses. People took pride in being Americans and in their personal appearance. Contrast that to today, when pants are worn mid-thigh, tattoos over much of the body, metal in lips, eye lids and ears, among other places. Many have no concern for their appearance, or their actions for that matter. We have become a decadent society and that is why those Democrat debates came as no surprise to me.

On stage, we found an elderly, self-proclaimed Democrat Socialist who would not rule out a 90% tax on American incomes, and who promised everything free; when anyone with an IQ higher than Jello knows that nothing is free. Somebody pays for it.

Beside the Democrat Socialist was someone who I believe to be the most corrupt, unethical liar in our history, Hillary Clinton. That's saying a lot considering Obama was in office at the time.

Bernie Sanders is a left-wing loon who believes that the United States must be like Denmark, Sweden and Norway; where government rules and citizens meekly obey. I have been to each of those countries more than once and walked and talked among common folks.

Again and again, I heard complaints about their lack of freedom, a tax system that demands more and more of their earnings, and their desire to get to the United States, the same United States that Bernie Sanders believes should be like their countries.

The real people in the rest of the world see America as their greatest hope, while Socialists and Communists in the Democrat party seek to destroy it.

During those debates, to Sanders' left stood a buffoonish Hillary Clinton, cackling like a Canada Goose with a hernia, ducking and dodging questions with political talking points, yet she was not confronted by the host of CNN or by the other four so-called opponents on stage with her, including Sanders, as she made the most outrageous statements.

Three of the democrats on the debate stage were people with no hope of even coming close to winning the Democrat nomination for president. That left Sanders as Hillary's only competitor, and that is being kind. It was no debate. It was designed as a long commercial for Clinton.

Sanders made a big issue of telling the camera that Americans were tired of hearing about Hillary's emails. The room, packed with die hard Democrats erupted in applause. Meanwhile, the FBI was considering criminal charges against Clinton over those very same emails. An age-old trick in Washington politics involves stalling investigations as long as possible and then claiming that the American people have moved on.

Well, people had not moved on from Clinton's emails. This was not simply a "bad choice," as Hillary claimed, about using a private server that put America's security as risk. It was a deliberate action by Hillary Clinton to keep evidence of wrongdoing close at hand so that destroying it is easier. She and Bill have used such tactics many, many times and were able to escape their actions when evidence could not be found.

The only time they miscalculated was when Monica Lewinsky produced the blue dress that the Clintons didn't know she had kept. Hillary had been calling Lewinsky a crackpot, and worse, but once the evidence came forward both Clintons stopped the name calling.

Bill lied under oath and neither Bill nor Hillary have a license to practice law any longer.

Does that seem to bother Democrat supporters? Not in the least. Apparently, these gullible sheep would follow Hillary over a cliff and leave America with at least four more years of Barack Obama-style disasters. The more the senile Sanders veered to the extreme left, the more Hillary scurried to get further left, to placate today's Democrat base.

Of Hillary flip-flopped again and moved somewhat away from the left-wing loons. but she changed her positions so many times that it was difficult for people to believe she had any core values. In 2008, Hillary opposed same-sex marriage. She also supported the Second Amendment and stood behind her vote for war in Iraq. She also opposed driver's licenses for illegal aliens. During her campaign, she changed her mind on all of those issues in just one week. She was willing to do anything to keep power so that millions of dollars would keep pouring into that farce known as the Clinton Foundation, which, in reality, was a piggy bank for the Clinton family.

I'm thankful the people were wise enough to not put Clinton in the Oval Office. However, the battle for the hearts and minds of especially America's youth is still going on. We have not won the war. Our future voting citizens, indoctrinated at our colleges and universities by liberal professors, are easy prey for Progressives. This will make it easy for them to follow the yellow brick road to Socialism.

Decades ago, Alexis de Tocqueville said, "The American republic will endure until the day Congress discovers that it can bribe the public with the public's money."

That day arrived in the early 60s when Democrats put aside their Klan hoods and their attacks against blacks. They saw where their votes could be purchased with public money. Just make blacks, and poor whites, totally dependent on government handouts. Spread some walking around money among certain devious black pastors who would, and did, sell out their own people for pieces of silver. Make blacks believe that they are victims to keep unrest in the black community and then set back and watch self-appointed black leaders stoke the fires of hate and assure a Democrat vote on election day.

Those of you who have been registered Democrats in the past must understand that the party you thought you knew left you decades ago and has moved further and further to the extreme left. Take a look at the pitiful lineup of those representing today's Democrat party.

Begin with our previous president Barack Obama. It will take many years to repair the damage he has brought upon us. Then move to Hillary Clinton, whose lies and corruption know no bounds. If she was Pinocchio her snout would extend to China. Next, Bernie Sanders, an avowed Democrat Socialist. Folks, the Nazis were Democratic Socialists.

Take an honest look at Nancy Pelosi, a deranged California liberal whose home state has been destroyed by Democrat policies. Then consider the recently-retired Harry Reid, a man to whom lies, deceit and corruption are common place.

Another pride and joy of the Democrats is Elizabeth Warren, as far left as Sanders and who never met a giveaway of other people's money that she did not like.

The Democrat party is also home to true racists like Elijah Cummings, Maxine Waters, Charlie Rangel and Sheila Jackson-Lee, who has a liberal Yale degree but makes ignorant statements that a middle-school dropout would know not to utter.

The list goes on. There is John Conyers and Debbie Wasserman-Schultz, who is a Democrat leader who believes that the slaughter of babies is fine up to the day of birth, and worse, does not rule out killing the baby after birth.

Van Jones, was appointed as green czar by Obama, but who had to resign after he was caught with his hands in the political cookie jar. Add to the collection the California twins, Barbara Boxer and Diane Feinstein, as well as Rham Emanuel, the Democrat mayor of Chicago which is the snake pit of the country thanks to Democrat policies and "leadership."

Speaking of Chicago, the city's public school CEO, another Democrat, pled guilty to issuing $23 million worth of no-bid contracts for which she received kickbacks. Lisa Crinel, a New Orleans Democrat donor, just pled guilty to corruption. Both women are black Democrats who put themselves above the country, their state and the people.

I challenge anyone to sincerely examine the crop of today's Democrat "leaders" and see where the Constitution, or the words "liberty" or "patriot" means anything to them.

They seem not to care that our children, and their children will be left to pay the national debt, that now approaches $20 trillion.

Speaking of that national debt, what do the Democrats say is the solution? They NEVER mention cutting spending or tax relief. Instead, they cry for more and more taxes so they can continue to give more than Santa Claus to, in essence, buy votes. Even if we taxed everyone who made over a million dollars in this country at 100 percent, that would bring in only $616 billion, a far cry from the $20 trillion these greedy, power-hungry politicians have left us saddled with.

With all the serious issues we are leaving behind for our nation's youth to inherit, ranging from that unsustainable debt to the growing threat of radical Islamic terrorism, what do the Democrats believe is the number one threat to America? Global warming, the very thing that Al Gore said would have melted most of Alaska and put Manhattan under water by now.

Tom Joyner

Random Thoughts

.

Chapter Forty-Seven

As I ponder the many issues threatening the liberty, patriotism and future of America, there are a number of random thoughts that go through my head. Let me share of them with you.

The United States in hopelessly in debt. The $20 trillion debt talked about does not include unfunded liabilities; money we owe for certain programs like Medicare and Medicaid, but which is simply not there. When we add that in, our debt is closer to $80 trillion dollars. Today, 44 million Americans are getting food stamps. Too many are using these EBT funds to buy everything from cigarettes to booze to drugs. Scammers pay fifty cents on the dollar for food stamps and there is a long list of those trying to sell.

As *USA Today* pointed out, the supplemental nutrition assistance program, known as food stamps, would take one of the biggest hits in the new budget - $190 billion dollars over ten years. The cuts are intended to get able-bodied adults off of food stamps.

Barack Obama propelled us to 44 million Americans on food stamps. Somebody has to pay for those food stamps and it is the 50% of us today who are paying taxes. Republicans released their budget recently and it was met with the same old Democrat criticism about children dying and grandmas being starved to death. Such claims have become staples in the Democrat party's attacks. They are not only fake news but political games.

There is no cut in the budget, just a move to keep waste and fraud out, and eliminate those who are scamming the system. I'll give you an example of what liberal Democrats call a cut. Let's say a person asks for a raise of 10% and the company offers only 5%. In the world of liberal Democrats that is a pay cut.

I'll detail how some people...a lot of people...are getting food assistance or disability payments who should be working instead, and the federal government cannot afford to spend as much on health care programs for more than the most disadvantaged.

Our political system is set up for failure. We elect people to Congress who can only be reelected if they protect the interest of their constituents. So those from farm country look out for farmers, most of whom now are major corporations, and that is their only real concern. Others in Congress have different constituent concerns and so they are pitted against one another and nobody wants to curb their own spending.

Today, our weary taxpayers are asked to pay for arts that entail whatever gross projects are called "art." A cross on public display submerged in urine is one that is hard to forget. There is just so much that the taxpaying public can bear. Politics today reminds one of the how blind Congress is as it tries to buy power with the public purse. They know it can't go on forever, but they're only concerned with reelection, as long as the country lasts. That goes for Democrats and Republicans.

In the meantime, our children and grandchildren are being indoctrinated in schools and universities to see their own country as the greatest of the world's evils. It is time to stop worrying about the world we leave to our children and start worrying about the children we are leaving to the world.

Common sense is out the window. We have members of the gay community calling for cooperation with Islam, all the while Islam is killing gay people in horrendous ways. We have morons like Congresswoman Maxine waters calling for Sharia Law in the United States. Under Sharia, Waters would not be allowed in Congress, she would be relegated to a second-class citizen and have no voice in her future because she is a woman. The only good thing is that under Sharia, Waters would have a hood over her face and her ignorance would be relegated to silence.

We continue to see people trying to divide us. I watched a bit of the Senate Intelligence Committee's grilling of government security officials recently and the so-called hearing was another farce. This is the same committee that had now-former FBI Director James Comey testify before it.

It was apparent that the Democrats were trying to force these security officials into saying something that would be damaging to President Trump. When they refused to do so, these rabid liberal Democrats got nasty. Each of these officials offered to answer their loaded questions in a private hearing, but these Democrats kept trying to make them answer in public.

The reason for that is that they can then take the answer and skew it into a political attack against the President. The answers they sought were being offered, just not in a public forum for political purposes. That was not good enough for these demagogues. They pretended that the officials were not willing to answer, hence a coverup. Their answers would be promptly answered in a private setting.

This is the new norm in Washington. They don't want answers unless they fit within their agenda against the President. The Democrats tried to force Comey to say that the president obstructed justice by asking Comey a question about General Mike Flynn. Comey had already testified, under oath, that no one, including the president had ever obstructed justice. That was before Comey was fired as FBI director.

As I predicted, Comey split hairs and said President Trump inquired as to the seriousness of the charges against General Flynn. That, by the way, is normal behavior for a president to inquire about a member of his or her administration. Asking about how serious the charges against Flynn were, and whether or not they rise to the level of a continued investigation, is not obstruction of justice. Nor is it illegal in any way. Donald Trump is not a polished politician who has learned to use terms that give him cover. He is blunt and has no time for political games.

Why is this so important? Because it is dishonest and devious. Congress warned Hillary Clinton not to destroy evidence in her emails, but Clinton, after that warning, destroyed some 33,000 emails. She not only had them erased but she then hired someone to scrub her server clean. Why? If there was no incriminating evidence there, why scrub the server?

That my friends IS obstruction of justice in its most basic form, and yet these same rabid Democrats not only failed to call Clinton's hand on it, they actively sought ways to help her evade prosecution.

The American people deserve honesty in government, not this continued pattern of lies and deception.

Can we not see that this political gamesmanship is harmful for the country? Like him or not, Donald Trump has been running full speed to fulfill his promises to the American people who elected him. Democrats, meanwhile, pile on his back and grab his legs to slow his progress, all the while they accuse him of not getting things done fast enough. That is sheer hypocrisy and they know it but they are blinded by their greed for power.

Chapter Forty-Eight

More Random Thoughts

I have never claimed to be an academic. My knowledge, such as it is, is not confined to books, but from 75 years of life experience where I was not just carried along by the rapids, but learned to swim with the sharks. I've been known to misspell a word and, occasionally, I might be caught using an improper tense.

Overeducated folks look down their noses at those of us who rely more on what we learned through life experiences than the hours spent in a classroom listening to a pompous, liberal, ponytailed professor, who cannot do and thus they teach. Take them out of the classroom and they have trouble finding a light switch.

Books have always been a part of my life and I continue to learn through them, but I've found that experience is worth more than a thousand words. Am I being a bit hard on tenured professors? Not all of them, of course, but the increasing numbers of them who choose to indoctrinate the young minds that come to them with liberal hogwash. It is they who have done more to destroy us from within.

It is interesting that Americans identify an expert or enlightened person as someone from out of town. We can't seem to comprehend that the man or woman we knew in middle school or high school can be the same person who; through dedication, perseverance, and a thirst for knowledge; can be that person from out of town.

All men and women begin as babes in the cradle. Some of us learned to walk and talk early and some of us later. All of us were given talents by God. Each one of us is unique. Sadly, most never realize their potential for a variety of reasons. They find reasons why others are at fault for their own failures. I've heard all of the excuses and I reject them all.

Yes, it is harder to succeed if you are poor, if you are a minority, if you have a handicap, but using that to excuse yourself is more harmful than the conditions you find yourself in. I get so frustrated when I see people who have one year's experience twenty times. Knowledge does not come from just listening, it comes from committing what you hear to your memory bank and acting on that knowledge.

I grew up with baloney sandwiches and roasted wieners. We had one fork and one spoon each at mealtime. When I left the Navy to work briefly at a newspaper in Rocky Mount, N.C., I was assigned to cover a formal dinner where there were formal place settings. Wine glass, water glass, tea glass, salad fork and all the rest. In such surroundings, it is important not to panic, but to learn by watching others and that's what I did. But I didn't just play copy-cat, I committed it all to my memory bank so that it was a learning experience that would not be wasted.

That is the way to approach all of the events in life. Listen or watch, commit to memory, and move on to the next experience. It's a slower process than going to finishing school perhaps, but when you're at the back of the line there is educational value in watching those ahead of you and avoiding the errors they make. Get your education wherever you find it and let not a minute go to waste. For those who think that advice is simplistic, I'll give you the numbers of my banker and broker.

Today, a rational person cannot possibly look at the rapid descent of the culture of the United States and not feel frustrated at best and despondent at worst. Common sense things that my generation took for granted are no longer considered common sense by a growing number of younger Americans.

How could our society have fallen so far so quickly? From the time I was a small boy I have heard Communists abroad and here at home tell us that they will bring us down. Not by war, but from the inside where we tear ourselves apart. Many Americans ignored the warnings and others felt that it could never happen to us. I'm sure that is how the Romans felt when their Empire ruled the world and felt invincible.

Their fall was a warning to the rest of civilization.

America is the greatest land of freedom the world has ever known, but we are not invincible. The very freedoms that we enjoy are used against us by who we welcome into our country and who have no intention of assimilating into our culture or embracing our customs. We have immigrants, legal and illegal, who march in our streets under a foreign flag and demand that we change our customs to mirror the country they fled from when they asked us for refuge. We have illegal immigrants demanding their rights when they have none, and a host of useful idiot citizens of our own country who join them.

We have professional protestors who are financed by Communist/Socialist billionaires in America, people like George Soros, who constantly organize protest marches about things they know nothing about. Idealistic college kids, indoctrinated at school, fall in behind the paid protestors with no sense of the real motives behind these marches.

A case in point was the healthcare draft that the Republicans in the Senate put forth last June. Democrats like Chuck Schumer and Nancy Pelosi had prepared disparaging remarks even before they knew what was in the draft. The moment the draft was presented these Democratic leaders were on television attacking it. They had offered no ideas of their own to save this country from a collapsing Obamacare plan that they had passed without reading, but were quick to attack the Republican plan that they had not read. Their opposition led them to asinine statements about people dying because of the Republican proposal.

That has long been the line of attack that floundering Democrats use to obstruct. Republicans want dirty air and dirty water. Republicans want to kill grandma. Read that again. Can you not see how juvenile it is? Republicans have children and grandchildren, just as Democrats do, and it is folly to suggest that Republicans want to breathe dirty air and drink dirty water. Republicans also have grandmas and how ignorant is it to claim that they want to kill them?

If Democrats had a plan to correct the course of Obamacare, a course that is not sustainable, that would be one thing, but for more than seven years they have watched the signs of this failing Obamacare plan and have done nothing to correct it. When Nancy Pelosi famously said that Democrats had to pass Obamacare to find out what was in it the mainstream media just smiled and ignored the comment. Ignorant comments deserve to be condemned when uttered. It is not enough to just poke holes in the other party's ideas, it is imperative that the critics present a better plan. That, the Democrats have not done. All of this jockeying for political power between our two major political parties contributes to destroying us from within.

About a decade or so ago we began on a journey to political correctness, a journey that continues today and contributes to our destruction from within. Words have been taken from our language because someone if offended by them. Free speech has become that speech that is approved by the liberal language posse.

As kids, we were taught that words can't harm us. Sure, some words may hurt your feelings, but we were taught to stay away from people uttering those words. Today, young snowflakes wear their feelings on their sleeves. Place your hand upon another person's hand and you've committed assault. In a Pennsylvania college, a co-ed filed a lawsuit against a boy who called her a water buffalo. Obviously, it is rude to call someone a water buffalo but the offended person knows they are not a water buffalo and nobody else cares.

I never use the "N" word because I am sensitive to the feelings of blacks who see that word as derogatory and because there is some history to back up their claim; but if we have the free speech that liberals demand for themselves, why is that word or others deleted? I don't advocate for using the "N" word and when I hear someone using it I cringe, but when was it decided that someone else gets to tell me what free speech I can use?

I'm also amazed at the hypocrisy of liberal college students who welcome liberal speakers on campus, but riot and protest Conservatives who wish to speak on campus, even those who have been invited. Liberals claim that Conservatives are stuck in the past, but it pays to revisit the past if only to see what the future became. All of this contributes to the destruction of America from within.

I don't have insurance with Progressive, but if I did, their phone would ring and I'd be on the cancel list.

The TV commercial they are running is offensive to me and should to offensive to any parent. Parents are mocked in the ad and Progressive tells the younger generation that they can't stop them from turning out like their parents, but buy their insurance anyway. That simply adds to the liberal narrative that these sniveling snowflakes are so much smarter than their parents and it would be a shame for them to turn out like their parents.

I'm proud to be my Mother and Father's son. They were not among the over-educated elitists whose liberal views have America on a fast track to oblivion, but they were honest, hard-working people who loved their country and, in my father's case, served in our military. They stayed together and loved their children. All of us were taught to treat a janitor with the same respect we gave to the bank president, and God was kept alive in our home.

Sorry Progressive, I am proud to have become my parents.

Chapter Forty-Nine

We all have hidden talents, but many Americans never discover those talents and there are several reasons why. Great success in life is hard. Amassing enough money to be financially independent is hard and keeping what you've earned is even harder.

Early pregnancies derail hopes and dreams. Going into debt keeps one from being able to move to where better opportunities might be. Fear is a great factor in convincing one to accept the status quo and not take risks in the job market.

One of the great job market opportunities sprung up a few years ago when oil took North Dakota to the forefront of energy supplies in this country. They were desperate for workers to fill the jobs. Not just in the oil fields, but in surrounding businesses. It was a great opportunity to start a small business or get experience that could lead to being your own boss, but many potential job applicants didn't want to travel to or live in North Dakota.

I cannot answer for others, I can only offer up my own experiences on the trail to a better life. I took many roads on that journey and risked all that I had time and again.

I remember back in 1963 when I was offered a better job at KEWI in Topeka, Kansas. I was in Durham, N.C. at the time and had just eight months experience in radio. The idea of pulling up and driving to Kansas was scary. What if I failed? It took all the strength that I could muster to make that move. As I got closer to Topeka, I picked up the radio station on my AM car radio and heard the most booming voice I had ever experienced. It was a man named Craig Deitschmann, but his on-air name was Richard C. Douglas. He did the production voiceovers for the station and his power and professionalism told me that I was about to get into a talent pool that was way over my head. I honestly considered turning back to North Carolina, but summoned the courage to go on to Topeka.

Once I was on air at KEWI it was apparent that my southern drawl would not fly in the Midwest. I hunkered down to learn how to get all regionalism out of my voice. I worked on it day and night and before long I sounded as if I belonged in Kansas. I've continued to work on that delivery. Oddly enough, I sometimes find myself dropping back into my southern roots when speaking informally, but never on radio.

It's difficult to give advice to many young people today. Words like sacrifice, risk-versus-reward, practice, dedication and tomorrow fall on deaf ears. They want it all today, not tomorrow.

We have developed an instant gratification society. People today have no concept of what life was like for their parents and grandparents and they have little desire to understand it.

I used to sit with my grandfathers and listen intently to their wisdom that came from years of experience in life. Getting children or grandchildren to sit and listen today, after the age of 13, is like pulling teeth from a running mule. That's their loss because a treasure trove of information is available for them and left unheard.

I can remember when I was in my 20s being advised to save money for a rainy day and to plan for the future, but the future seemed so far away and I could not imagine giving up a hamburger today for a steak tomorrow. I wised up in my late 30s and began a discipline designed to make my family financially secure in later years. That takes will power just like stopping smoking or giving up alcohol.

Most Americans honestly believe that they have no money to save. Statistics show that most of us could not come up with one thousand dollars if pressed to do so and have less than that amount in savings.

People take on deductibles in order to afford insurance and yet they do not begin building a nest egg for when they might need the money to pay the deductible. If you have a $500.00 deductible on your insurance policy it should be imperative that you set aside that amount over time to cover it.

Even a dollar a week mounts up. I know a man who smokes two-to-three packs of cigarettes a day and drinks as much as a six-pack of beer every day of his life. Yet, he complains that he doesn't have the money for medical insurance or to build a savings account. Write down your expenses for a month and you'll be surprised at how much money you could put aside by a little financial discipline in your life. I learned these lessons the hard way. But, I didn't just learn them, I applied them and today I'm called "lucky."

Technical innovations have given us conveniences that we take for granted. I remember as a small boy being amazed at the idea that in the future we'd be able to turn on electricity with one finger.

Let me explain what life was like when I grew up. As a very young boy, we had no electricity in the house. We read by coal oil lamps. There was no indoor plumbing and so we relied on an outhouse for calls of nature, and first a well and then a pump outside for water. There was no air conditioning, we relied on fans. For heat, there was a potbellied stove in one room of the house which demanded wood or coal to heat a very limited area. The kitchen stove was wood-burning and so that was a chore to be done every day.

It was a hardscrabble life. Those who did not live through those times can't fully understand the hardships their parents and grandparents endured. We moved 36 times before I left for the Navy in October, 1960, at the age of 18. It was with that background that I embarked on a quest to improve not just my life, but the lives of my family.

For me, there was no safety net and no room for failure. I smile when I hear someone speak of "white privilege." The color of my skin or any other poor person is not a gateway to riches. The color that counts is green.

The advice I would give to any young person, or those not so young, is to use each day to gain knowledge. Do your job, whatever that job may be, to the very best of your ability and while doing that, keep your eyes open for other opportunities.

Most go through life with blinders on. Don't just walk through the paces, learn other aspects of the jobs in your company. I took significant decreases in pay to move from one position in radio to another so that in the end I would have the knowledge to run my own station if that opportunity ever presented itself. When that opportunity came, I was prepared.

Opportunity does not knock very often and when it does those who have not prepared themselves are passed over. I never considered myself working for a company. I worked for myself and if that benefitted the company we both won. When and if I ever left that company, I took all of the knowledge I had gained with me. So, those who complain about not being paid what they are worth should re-examine their goals. It's not today's paycheck that matters most, but the day when you use all of the knowledge you've gained to own your own business.

Chapter Forty-Nine

Final Thoughts

With more than fifty years in broadcasting behind me and being fortunate to have much success in the business, people have asked why I have not completely retired. Actually, I did retire. That was in 2014. It was the third time I had tried to "take it easy." My wife, Anne, knows me and didn't start packing.

Carl Lamm called. He is the long-time owner of WTSB Radio, serving the Selma-Smithfield, North Carolina area. He asked if I would come on his station and break down current events in a way the average, ordinary American could understand them.

I thought about it long and hard, because I had been charging uphill all of my adult life and, frankly, I was tired. After a few days my love and concern for my country overrode my need for rest and I agreed to do a commentary.

It was supposed to be a one-time appearance. The good listeners of WTSB, however, wanted more. So, that one-time appearance has grown into weekly commentaries every week, and sometimes more often when current issues warrant.

. I do an enormous amount of research for my commentaries because I value my credibility and because a mistake by an opinionated Conservative will bring down the wrath of liberals quicker than Hillary can erase emails.

Since WTSB streams live on the Internet, my commentaries can be heard worldwide. We have documented listeners as far west as Salem, Oregon, to the west and Miami, Florida in the south. We have listeners in New York and multiple other states.

I'm also heard on WFBT, known as "the Big Talker," in Wilmington, N.C. and make frequent appearances on the John Butler Book Program on WFLA in Orlando, Florida. In addition, I have a growing list of listeners who receive an email link to listen to commentaries online. That way, they can listen at their convenience. If you'd like to subscribe, simply drop a line to comments@tomjoyner.net. The response I get from listeners has become the wind beneath my wings.

As I was writing this book, I kept thinking of all the things I'd like to comment on, but the ink was limited and I chose to bring the comments to a close.

I cannot tell you how much it means to me for your support of my efforts on radio and in the purchase of this book. God has been extremely generous to me. Fifty-two years ago, he led me to my wife who has been a solid rock for me. She moved so many times when I was coming up in broadcasting that I threatened to buy us a U-Haul trailer and she never complained. When I told her on our first date that one day she'd be married to a millionaire I'm pretty sure that I meant someone else, but she persevered.

Our daughter, Lisa, is a beautiful and bright woman who could have had a career in music but chose to raise a family instead. Our son-in-law, Bob, is one of the best family men I've ever known and what more could a father ask?

We have two granddaughters, Anna Marie, who is a sophomore at Meredith College and who is on the Dean's list majoring in drama and in hotel management, with a minor in French. She speaks French fluently and is a deep-thinking woman with patience and grace.

Speaking of Grace, that's the name of my other granddaughter. She has just entered high school and was very active in elementary school. Grace is the athlete in the family (not withstanding her Papa's exploits in high school in baseball, football and basketball). She plays soccer, softball and runs track. Grace is a straight "A" student and a sweet, caring human being.

Of my five siblings, I have two left. William, who we call "Hot Shot," and my sister, Ann, who live in Goldsboro and we maintain a tight bond. Nobody knows your trials and tribulations like those who have known you since their birth.

Lastly, I'd like to acknowledge my dear friend Carl Lamm of WTSB in Selma/Smithfield. I greatly admire Carl and WTSB because they represent broadcasting as it was meant to be. Their focus is on the local community entirely. It is their dedication to local radio that drew me to them and keeps me on air. Carl is, I believe, the oldest broadcaster in North Carolina and perhaps the entire country as he approaches 90. His mind is sharp and his devotion to God is unshakable.

Carl's introductions to my commentaries are more than I deserve, but he alone has kept me interested in speaking out, as I have on radio and in this book.

Thanks for your attention and GOD BLESS AMERICA!

CPSIA information can be obtained
at www.ICGtesting.com
Printed in the USA
LVOW10s1032261217
560814LV00023B/448/P